*For anyone facing challenges or j[...]
a first-hand, feel-good, inspiring roadmap reminding us that getting the
seemingly "little things" right is actually the most crucial determinant of
achievement and fulfillment. It's also a wake-up call for anyone seeking
greater happiness and fulfillment in their lives that change is well within
our grasp with the right approach and attitude.*

—TIM LIPSKY, MBA
BRAND STRATEGY DIRECTOR, CO-FOUNDER SETTER ADVERTISING

*If success and self-care are on your to-do list this decade, From Despair To
Millionaire has all the tools you need to make it happen! If you're seeking
a well-balanced, easy-to-follow guide that can help anyone pick up the
pieces, financially and emotionally, look no further. Uplifting. Motivating.
Powerful. This book will change your life.*

—STACEY SARAKINIOTIS, M.ED, LMHC

*A nice blend of Eric's personal story and generalized advice. In particular, I
appreciated his thoughts on learning differences, mentors, and communication.*

—JONATHAN GREEN, M.ED.
DIRECTOR, HAMILTON SCHOOL AT WHEELER

*Don't be fooled by the cover. This is not another book about how to become
a millionaire. We are all, each of us, travelers in this journey we call life.
With an easy-to-read, disarmingly honest style, Eric shares his life story with
vulnerability and humility as he provides a host of pragmatic, actionable
"life lessons" that you can use on your own road to success, whatever you
define that to be. Eric reminds us that no matter what challenges we may
face, happiness and fulfillment are attainable for us all.*

—MARK STROZIK, SPHR, SCP
C-SUITE HR EXECUTIVE CERTIFIED COACH

Wealth is not always about money. Wealth is also demonstrated in the form of strong and meaningful relationships based on integrity, respect, and kind lovingness. In Chasen's easy-to-digest yet powerful book, he gives us the blueprint for creating and maintaining those relationships—with self, others, and society in general. He illuminates the importance of building character as a way of building success in all areas of our lives. Chasen shares his knowledge, passion, and keen insight in this book and serves as a mentor to anyone who wishes to move ahead in life.

—PAUL SILVA, CPC, ELI-MP, ACC
ADDICTION RECOVERY AND LIFE TRANSITION COACH

From Despair To Millionaire gives you basic but unique tools that will have a direct and immediate impact on your future. No matter what stage in your career you are in—just starting out or contemplating a new chapter, Eric inspires you to get out of your own way. He breaks it all down into simple, tangible steps. Thank you, Eric, for sharing your story in such a brave, vulnerable, and bold way!

—KRISTIN TODD, VICE PRESIDENT OF MARKETING,
CFO LEADERSHIP COUNCIL MARKETING ENTHUSIAST, STRATEGIC NETWORKER

From Despair to Millionaire is a formidable contribution to the leadership literature and an indispensable read for those interested in living an authentic and successful life. Through personal challenges and triumphs, Eric embraces life's lessons and in doing so emerges on a path to a life filled with purpose, meaning, and success. Read this book, re-read this book, and give it to friends who have the courage to know who they are and desire to create a big life for themselves. Better yet, while you still can, hire him as your coach—he will help you turn things around, find the next step, and live your best life!

—JEANNETTE DE JESÚS, MSW, MPA
CEO & FOUNDER STRATEGIC MOVES LLC

from
DESPAIR *to*
MILLIONAIRE

Growing Beyond Hardship

ERIC CHASEN

From Despair to Millionaire
Growing Beyond Hardship

Eric Chasen

FIRST EDITION

ISBN: 978-1-7347104-0-3
eBook ISBN: 978-1-7347104-1-0

Library of Congress Control Number: 2020903946

Atibelcom Publishing, LLC

The information in this book is neither intended nor implied to be a substitute
for professional, psychological, medical, or legal advice. All content is for general
purposes only. The author makes no representations and assumes no responsibility
for the accuracy or efficacy of the information herein and shall have no liability
for any damages, loss, or injury from reliance on the information herein.

To my son, Alex.
May you continue to have a life
filled with good health and happiness

CONTENTS

Foreword   ix

Introduction   xi

Chapter 1   A Good Candidate   1

Chapter 2   Vulnerable. And Strong.   9

Chapter 3   Mentors: Pathways to Success   19

Chapter 4   The Intangibles   33

Chapter 5   Treating Others Well:
            The Best Investment You Can Make in Yourself   45

Chapter 6   Communication:
            The Foundation of Everything People Related   59

Chapter 7   Gratitude: The Key to Fulfillment   75

Chapter 8   The Thing about Luck   87

Chapter 9   Perspective   99

Chapter 10 Paying it Forward   111

Chapter 11 Moving Beyond "Success"   121

Chapter 12 Resiliency, Guts, and Grit   133

Final Thoughts   141

Points to Ponder   145

About the Author   157

FOREWORD

Eric will tell you in this book about the death of our mother. I have my own recollection. When the time was getting near, she told me privately that she was concerned about Eric. He was just starting out in his career and, as you'll learn, he had just gone through some very tough times. I'm ten years older than Eric and he'd always looked up to me. I told our mother not to worry; I would always make sure Eric was okay.

I got the chance to keep that promise when I started Triton Technologies. I brought Eric in as a partner. But it was far from charity or even brotherly love. I knew our new company needed what Eric could bring to the table. I knew of his work ethic. I knew of his dedication and commitment. Mostly, I knew of his leadership skills. He's one of those guys that people just sort of want to follow. He motivates and inspires. I felt it myself. He looked up to me? Heck, I looked up to him.

We took a trip to Vegas where we played a little blackjack and I wrote up a business plan. Eric knew the industry and we decided that, as a means by which to differentiate ourselves, we'd position our company as performance-based, promising to deliver "ultimate" performance.

Eric was the perfect guy to make this happen. Over time, he built an amazing call center sales team, hiring the right people and then motivating them to go beyond themselves. He chose ethical people. That was always important to us. In the hiring process, he tested their interest and work habits by purposely scheduling a second interview, even if he had nothing further to ask. He just wanted to make sure they'd come back and that they'd come back on time. That would tell him more than anything else about the potential applicant's work ethic.

Once hired, those employees would find Eric demanding, but fair. If you weren't working up to his standards, you'd first get a verbal warning, then a written one. There would often be no third warning. But Eric made it fun, too. There was a great deal of camaraderie in the call center—the engine room as I used to call it. People responded to Eric's leadership style and he got more out of them than anybody else could have ever gotten. He made it all happen and I slept easier at night knowing Eric was in charge of the engine room.

I don't want to suggest we never had any disagreements. But early on, I brought Eric into my office and we talked and both agreed that the business would never come between our brotherhood and our friendship. And it never did. The business, as successful as it became, could never be as important to me as our relationship.

If you're looking for a little help in your life or career, I can't think of a better person to listen to than Eric. Wherever you are in life, Eric's probably been there. You'll read in this book about his struggles and you'll come to understand why he calls himself a "resilience" coach. This isn't a book of theory. This is a book of facts.

The lessons that Eric has learned along the way work. I know. I've seen it firsthand. And I can't think of a better guy to learn from. A guy I admire—my brother and my friend.

Steve Chasen
April 2020

INTRODUCTION

It's a truism that nothing worthwhile ever comes without a little hardship along the way. Sometimes, a lot of hardship. We forget this, however, in the course of our daily lives. We get comfortable and settle into routines and feel as if everything is supposed to go our way. But then, when something unfortunate happens—a tragedy or a career setback or financial problems—we get shaken out of our comfort and think about how unfair life is. But life is neither fair nor unfair. Life is life—full of ups and downs and in-betweens. There are pitfalls and detours that come along with the easy stretches. The key is to be able to absorb it all and keep moving forward.

This book is about the hardships. As you'll read, I have experienced my share of them. I've been in places of complete despair. But over the years, I have grown to appreciate the hardships. Not for the difficulties they brought me, but for the opportunities they helped forge—opportunities for me to learn and grow and become a better person.

This book is also about that growth. In my career, I grew beyond the hardships and attained a level of success I would not have thought possible based on where I started. If you had told me I would someday have in life what I now have, I'd have said you were insane. But it happened. Often, as I climbed up first out of my despair and then into real success, people would ask me what my "secret" was. After I retired, a *lot* of people asked. I was still relatively young, after all. How had I done it?

It might seem funny, but through my working years, I never really stopped to consider how I had accomplished what I'd accomplished. I'd been too busy to stop and analyze my success. I just kept going, kept working, kept putting one foot in front of the other. Now, with time on my hands, I decided to seriously consider the question. Maybe if I could determine what my secret to success was, I could help other people succeed.

I took many months examining my career, scrutinizing it, looking for clues, trying to find that one secret that I could pass along. I mentally re-lived certain events and turning points and influential factors. I came up empty. I couldn't find "the secret." Maybe, after all, it was just luck, I thought.

But then I looked even harder. Or, really, I stopped looking and started thinking. I stepped back from my life and career to consider everything a little more objectively. And one day, it struck me like a lightning bolt. What I came to see was that there was no one "secret." Instead, there were a lot of little things, none of which are secrets and most of which are, in fact, common sense. This should not have come as a surprise to me. All during my career, I strove to do things the right way, never to cut corners or look for shortcuts that could substitute for good, old-fashioned hard work. So why would I look for some secret shortcut now?

The good news is that although success depends on many things, those things are really pretty simple. Over the years, some came to me easily. Others took a lot of work. But even the harder ones were simple in their essence. Hard doesn't have to mean complex. There's nothing in my success that's mysterious or complicated. It's all out there. There's nothing to invent. And if I could do it, you can do it, too. The power or "the secret" is found in the simple, the basic, and in the ordinary rising to extraordinary.

In the course of preparing the material for this book, I have thought a lot about all of the things that helped me succeed. And then I took those things and put them into an order that I think makes sense. The result is the book you hold in your hands. Within these pages, you will learn about the strength required to ask for help in the first place, about mentors and mentoring, the importance of an open-mind toward learning, certain intangible qualities that define the attitude of a successful person, confidence and its relationship to humility, kindness and other things we learned in kindergarten but forgot, communication skills, gratitude, preparation, perspective, expectations, goal-setting, and resilience.

If this sounds like it's a bit all over the boards, well it is. And yet all of this, as you'll see in the course of this book, is related. One thing feeds off another. Communication skills, for instance, don't work without kindness. Goal-setting is an exercise in futility without perspective. Learning doesn't take place without humility.

Here are some things that aren't necessary for success: a lot of money, a high level of education, important connections, blind luck. These can all help, of course, but I had none of them. In fact, I would argue that even with these advantages, success can be elusive without the qualities you'll see outlined in this book. So, if you're starting out and you don't have a lot of money, you don't have an MBA, you don't have a rich uncle who's going to give you a plumb job in his corporation, and you don't have a winning lottery ticket in your pocket, then rest easy. You're right where most of us start out. And you're going to be just fine. All you need is a willingness to learn and picking up this book is evidence that you already have that.

Which brings me to how the book ought to be read. I think you'll be pleased with the amount of information in this book. It's thirty years of what I'd learned over my career. And yet, I've kept it fairly short and compact and tried to write it in such a way so as to keep the material flowing well. Learning about how to be successful shouldn't be overwhelming or laborious. It shouldn't require a ponderous, weighty tome full of tedious and tiresome reading. But though this book is easy reading, don't get lulled into the idea of simply reading it from one end to the other as quickly as you can. There are ideas in this book that are meant to be contemplated, even internalized. If you come upon an idea that resonates with you, or an idea you want to think over a little more, it's okay to put the book down and contemplate what you just read for a little while. Meditate on it. Carry the thought around with you for a day or so. And then come back to the book. You won't get points for how fast you can read this book. You'll get far more out of it by thinking the material over.

I say this because although I can present any given idea, I can't apply it directly to your life or career. Only you can do that. Only you can decide how best to implement a suggestion you might find herein. Only you can take the general to the specific, as it relates to you and your life. The material in this book, in and of itself, is theoretical. Until, that is, it's implemented. Then it becomes very real. But I can't implement it for you. You have to figure out how to do that, and that means thinking about this material and seeing how you can relate it to your own very specific, very personal, situation. And you can't do that by glossing over it.

Everyone's approach to the use of this material will be different because everyone's situation is a little different. So read this whole book through in a hurry if you must. But then read it again, slowly and more deliberately. Use a highlighter. Bookmark the pages. Underline the passages that you really want to remember. Let the material sink in.

I'm sure you'll get at least something out of this book that you can carry with you into your life. Hopefully, you'll get a lot out of it. I can recommend the ideas you're going to read about because they worked for me and I had absolutely nothing that you don't have. You can do it. You can succeed. You can make your dreams come through.

And that's another very personal aspect. This isn't a book about how to become a millionaire. I became one, but that was never my goal. As you'll read, I wanted to be a success in my field. I loved the work for its own sake, just as I love my current work as an author, mentor, and coach. But money, I have learned, has a tendency to follow success no matter the field. It can follow you, too, and then you'll be free to pursue those things that bring you fulfillment, which may be your work, or it may be something else. For me, fulfillment includes work, but it also includes family and, importantly, the increase in options that comes with freedom of choice. Whatever fulfillment means to you, in the end, that's really what it's all about. That's what we're all looking for. My hope is that I can help you get there. I know it's possible. In fact, it's more than possible. And you deserve it just as much as me.

ONE

A GOOD CANDIDATE

"Just as despair can come to one only from other human beings, hope too, can be given to one only by other human beings."

— Elie Weisel —

The period of late 1998/early 1999 might have been the best time of my life. In October of 1998, on the observation deck of the Stratosphere Hotel, 1,149 feet above the city of Las Vegas, I proposed to Jennifer. We'd been dating for a few months. Jen was the closest I'd ever come to love at first sight and I knew she was the woman I wanted to spend the rest of my life with. She was warm and wonderful and everything I could ask for.

I had met Jen at the phone sales company I worked for in a job in which I excelled. I'd found my area of expertise and the future was bright. Career, personal life—I was the luckiest guy in the world. Jen said yes on that observation deck and we set a wedding date for July of 1999.

In early '99, things became even more exciting. Yes, the job at Talk America had been great, but I received an offer with a heck of a lot more upside—a startup company wanted to bring me in to help build out their call center. I'd be responsible for interviewing, training, and managing our sales agents. The initial pay would be a step down for me. It was a startup, after all, so it was a startup wage. But now I'd have a small piece of the action—an actual equity position. It was an investment in the future, mine and Jen's. I took the offer and resolved to tighten my belt until things would take off, certain that they would.

The future never looked better.

Jen and I continued making our wedding plans. On a Saturday in April, Jen picked out her wedding gown. The next evening, she went out to the movies while I stayed behind in the townhouse we shared. But Jen never made it to the movies. About an hour and a half after she left, there was a knock on the door. Two police officers. They asked a few questions. "Are you Jennifer's husband?" I told them I was her fiancé. "Was she driving a van this evening?" Yes, I said. Then, when I invited the officers in, they suggested it might be a good idea if I was to sit down.

It was a single-car accident on a lonely country road that ran between Cumberland and Yarmouth, Maine. Jen's car had left the road and hit a tree. Nobody saw or will ever know exactly how it happened. There was speculation that maybe she'd swerved to avoid hitting a deer. However it happened, Jen left behind two daughters from a previous marriage, nine and seven years old. I had become very close to them over our relatively short time together.

I had no frame of reference for how to deal with the loss of my fiancé. It was unlike any loss I had ever experienced. I spent the next weeks and months in a state of disbelief and confusion. The first week, my brother Steve stayed with me. As it happened, he and my nephew were up visiting the weekend of the crash and had even been with us when we'd stopped by the bridal shop that Saturday for Jen to run in and make the final arrangements for her gown. They'd left Sunday, driving two and a half hours back to their home in Massachusetts. When I called Steve to tell him the news, he jumped right back in his car and came back to stay with me.

It was all horrifying and surreal. From hearing the news, to having to tell Jen's mother by phone with the police officers by my side in the condo, to calling my family, and then seeing the faces of Jen's daughters the next morning. It was a feeling beyond explanation.

My mother stayed with me the second week. I had always been close to my mother. I was the youngest of five—her "baby."

Mom had suffered loss in her life, too. My older brother, David, had been killed riding his bike at the age of thirteen. I hadn't been born yet. My eldest sister, eleven at the time of the death, remembers my mother's pragmatic strength: "You have to be grateful for the eleven years you had with him," my mother would tell her.

I asked Mom how she dealt with David's death. "How do you get over something like this?" I said in the midst of my own grief.

"You don't ever get over it, Eric," she said. "You just learn to live with it." Mom had done just that. She had learned to live with the death of her son. She was the pillar of our family. And through the dark days following Jen's death, she was my rock. She would meet me at the door of the condo each day when I came home from work during that first week back. What would I have done without her during those early, indescribably difficult days?

I threw myself into my work, but things with the startup were only just ramping up. This should not have been entirely surprising. New businesses take time. But the startup was taking more time than I had anticipated. My startup salary wasn't enough to make ends meet. In fact, it wasn't even close. I soon found myself in debt and the debt continued to accumulate.

More than once, to make it between paychecks, I found myself selling valuables to a local pawn shop. All it did was postpone the inevitable. I was in a hole from which I could see no way out. I consulted with a bankruptcy attorney. In retrospect, maybe I could have set up payment plans of some sort with my creditors, but I was crippled by my grief and I needed a simpler out. I declared bankruptcy in January of 2000.

I knew the bankruptcy would follow me for years, a stain on my credit. And there was no escaping the feeling of abject failure that bankruptcy brings about. Coupled with the loss of Jen, I fell into a depression. A deep depression. A psychologist I saw for a brief period around that time put it like this: "Eric, with everything you've been through recently, you'd be a good candidate for suicide."

The liquidation of my remaining assets at least cleared away my debts and I felt as if I could breathe again; a little, anyway. But if I felt anything akin to optimism, the feeling would not last. In fact, things were about to take a big turn for the worse. In March of that year (2000), Mom, seventy-five years old and an ex-heavy-smoker, having quit smoking some twenty years prior, went to the doctor complaining of wheezing and shortness of breath. She called me the day she received the results of her scope biopsy. "It's not good," she said.

The doctor said that Mom's lung cancer would permit her anywhere from six months to two years. All I heard was the two years and, like Mom, I remained optimistic. I can recall her stoic approach as she fought the cancer with both radiation and chemo, assuring me all would be okay, but acknowledging that no one lives forever. Mom spent the last month of her life in the hospital. Even just a week before her passing, she told them at the hospital that she'd be driving again soon. She made it for just five months after her diagnosis. Just like that, I lost my rock. I would somehow have to learn to live with Mom's death even though I still hadn't quite learned to live with Jen's.

I remembered what the psychologist had told me about being a candidate for suicide, but I never quite felt that. I never quite felt as if ending it was the right choice. I felt beaten, certainly. I felt defeated. I frequently felt lonely and isolated. I felt alienated from other people, people whose lives seemed to be clicking along nicely. Some days, I felt as if there was no hope at all. A promising future wasn't anything I could imagine. Success? Inconceivable. Happiness? Impossible. All I could manage was to put one foot in front of the other. Success for me back then meant just trying to get myself through each day.

But that much I did. And over time—and it was not a short time—a strange and wonderful thing happened. I began to feel hope again. Real and genuine hope. Even better, I found my determination again. I was young, after all. I had the rest of my life ahead of me. I needed to resist the natural inclination I'd had to simply get through each day, watching carelessly the weeks and months slip past. Life had meaning. Deep down, I knew it did. And I had to find it. I had to create it. I needed to make something of myself. The rest of my life was beckoning and it was up to me to grab a hold of it.

I can't say there was a specific day when all this occurred to me. I suppose it was a revelation that came to me slowly over weeks and months. Somewhere in that time, I changed. Or—maybe—I got back to the person I'd always been. However you want to say it, I moved forward again. I took Mom's advice and I learned to live with the tragedies and defeats. More precisely, I learned *from* them. And what I've learned has made all the difference. Who could have imagined the meteoric rise in my career and life since then? Retirement in my forties. Love and the blessing of having a son. A life of meaning, once again. The inconceivable became reality. The impossible became possible.

It's been a hell of a road. And as I look back on it all now, I can't help but see the many lessons that presented themselves along the way, lessons I couldn't even see at the time, but lessons that seem so clear to me now. I'm grateful for all of them. Gratitude, in fact, has been one of those lessons. But there is so much more to share. So many lessons that can lead to success and fulfillment. It's almost hard to know where to start. But, if you'll indulge me, I'd sure like to give it a try.

TWO

VULNERABLE. AND STRONG.

"You never get over it. You just learn to live with it."

— RHODA CHASEN, 1924-2000 —

My mother stayed with me for a week after Jen died and her presence provided enormous comfort. But, like my brother, who had stayed with me the week prior, she couldn't stay with me forever. They both had their own lives to attend to and I couldn't ask them to endlessly hang around. Both returned to Massachusetts and I found myself alone.

I didn't really know how to handle my grief at that point. I'd never experienced anything like it and didn't even know where to start. Fortunately, I was smart enough to know that. In other words, I was smart enough to know that *I didn't know*. I knew that I needed help. I wasn't strong enough to carry the load all by myself.

Almost right away, I joined a grief support group. It was held at the church in town where Jen's memorial service had been and there were ten in the group. The meetings were facilitated by a woman who had lost her husband several years before, a prominent physician in the area who had also died young. All the group members had lost spouses. I was the youngest in the group and the only one who had lost a fiancé. Everyone shared their experiences of loss and the feelings they were dealing with. It was comforting to know I was not alone in my grief, that others knew how I felt. There were eight sessions and these get-togethers helped, at least a little.

I read several books in this time, too. Books on grief like *How to go on Living when Someone You Love Dies* by Therese Rando and *When Bad Things Happen to Good People* by Rabbi Harold Kushner. These helped a little, too.

A board member of the start-up company was a retired psychologist and he recommended a fellow psychologist. This is the one I saw, the one who told me I was a potential candidate for suicide. He was competent enough but I saw him for only three sessions. One of the issues I was struggling with was survivor's guilt. I kept asking myself if there was something I could have done to prevent the tragedy. Maybe I shouldn't have let Jen go out to the movies by herself. Maybe I should have gone along. Maybe I should have convinced her to stay in. If I had done this or done that, maybe Jen would still be alive. The psychologist helped me a bit with this, but overall I didn't feel as though we were making the progress I needed and I stopped seeing him.

The fact is, I missed Jen. It was no more complicated than that. I missed how she made me feel and I wanted that feeling back. I *needed* that feeling back. So much so, in fact, that no more than three months after Jen's death, I signed up with a dating service. This was before online dating made its appearance. You filled out an in-depth questionnaire and sat for a long interview. Then the service paired you with someone they felt you matched up with. I had two dates and on both, I was candid about my recent loss, telling both women that if a relationship like what I had with Jen could happen once, maybe it could happen again. I needed to get back what I'd lost. Both women were equally candid with me: they were aghast that I was dating so soon! Needless to say, neither date led to a second one.

Because Jen had left two children behind, I thought it would be a good idea if I was to volunteer with the Center for Grieving Children, an organization that I found in Portland, Maine that helped kids who were going through the grief of losing someone. This would be a way, I thought, to channel my own grief into something positive, a way to move forward once again. But the people at the center would not accept my application, thanking me for wanting to help, but telling me that my own loss had come too soon prior to my volunteering. They preferred at least six months. A person should work through his or her own grief before trying to help or support others, they explained.

As it turns out, they were absolutely right. My real problem was that I *hadn't* worked through my grief. Eventually, it struck me that everything I had been doing, I had been doing to *not* deal with my grief. I'd been working to avoid it, to skirt around it, to shortcut the process necessary to come to terms with it. I wasn't processing Jen's death; I was trying to put it behind me. This was a mistake. Well-intentioned, perhaps, and coming from a place of genuine grief, but a mistake nonetheless.

I'd been smart enough to seek help—in groups and books and therapy and potential volunteer work—but I hadn't been smart enough to seek the right help for the right reasons at the right time. What I would eventually learn was that the tragedies and setbacks of a person's life cannot be sidestepped. They can't be avoided or hastily moved on from. Not for a person's long-term emotional health. Tragedies and setbacks need to be confronted. I look back now and wince at the idea that I thought I could get back the feeling I'd had with Jen by finding another woman through a dating service.

What I had with Jen had vanished in an instant. It was perfectly understandable, then, that I felt I needed it back, but I needed it back so desperately that I was unwilling to face its loss in the first place. In little ways, I suppose I tried. I moved out of what had been Jen's townhouse, and in my new place I set up a small shrine with pictures of Jen and some mementos of our time together. This was my way of dealing with the loss. It was comforting, but what I would ultimately come to realize was that the real process of grieving is helped by only one thing: time. And it cannot be accelerated. It moves at its own pace and it's not a pace that you can set. It's not a process that can be sped up or rushed.

What I needed was to not just face the loss, but to *live* with it, as my mother had told me all along. It had all been like a blur to me and I needed not to speed things up, but to slow things down. I needed to internalize what had happened in my life. My relationship with Jen was unique and could never be duplicated, and processing this would not be an overnight proposition.

I needed time.

But, of course, I didn't have a lot of that before I lost my mother. Now I had two monumental losses to confront.

Mom's loss wasn't as quick. I spent months running back and forth on weekends between Maine and Massachusetts seeing her in the hospital, clinging to the optimistic end of the range of time the doctor had given us, hoping we had that two years. But we didn't even make it to the lower end of six months.

At the time of Mom's death, my father was in a nursing home. He'd moved there due to severe arthritis, plus he'd become unstable on his feet. He would fall often. His cognitive abilities were on a steady decline as well. We'd always assumed Mom would outlive Dad. She'd been the healthy one and most of the women on her side of the family had lived well into their eighties and nineties. Sure, she'd smoked but that was a long time ago. We were never really sure what Dad knew and understood, but on the day before my mother died, my brother and I visited him to tell him Mom was dying. We made a little awkward small talk and then hemmed and hawed about Mom. Finally, in a moment of surprising clarity, our father said, "What's going on, guys? I know something's up." We told him about Mom and then, with a rented wheelchair van, we took him to see her. She died the next day. Dad would live for three more years but quickly slid downhill after Mom's death.

The loss of my mother was a different kind of loss than the loss of Jen, but both losses were devastating. Together, they went well beyond devastating. They were shattering. In my dreams, I'd had visions of a life with Jen, and sometimes those dreams included children, children that my mother would spoil as all grandmothers do. Now all of that was gone. No wife, no children, no grandmother.

Once again, the only ally I had was time.

In both cases, I was helped by the support of other loved ones, especially those who understood firsthand the losses. Jen's family was suffering every bit as much as I was, if not more. And her ex-husband and his wife were kind, gracious, and very understanding, often letting me continue to spend time with Jen's girls. This was important. Losing my access to the girls would have just compounded my grief. With Mom, I had the support of my siblings who all knew exactly how I felt. We could all lean on each other and help each other.

With Jen's death, I'd learned that I needed patience because the processing of grief requires time. With both deaths, I learned that it was okay to be vulnerable. I did not have to be afraid to show vulnerability around my loved ones. I could be open with them about how I felt because they felt it, too. This might have been the most helpful thing of all.

I say this because it seems to me that perhaps the biggest obstacle to healing is denying the pain, to yourself or to others. I began healing from the awful blow of Jen's death when I began to accept the pain and allow myself to be vulnerable to it, rather than avoid it as I had initially tried to do. Facing it meant leaving myself exposed and, at first, that was a difficult thing to do. And a little scary. But to be vulnerable is to be human and once you accept the vulnerability, you can ask for help, the kind of help that you might really need, for the right reasons and at the right times. And those reasons have to do with processing your grief, not with trying to find a "solution" to it, as had been my first recourse. Or, for that matter, an escape from it. There was a right time for the support group, for the books, for the psychologist, for volunteer work, even for dating again. The problem was that I hadn't been ready for those things because I hadn't been ready to be vulnerable and face the pain.

This idea of being vulnerable takes strength and it takes even more strength to act on the vulnerability and ask for the help you need. Ironically, society has a way of making it seem as if asking for help is a sign of weakness. In reality, it's exactly the opposite. This seems counterintuitive. Vulnerability equals strength? In the right context, allowing yourself to be vulnerable is the strongest thing you can do.

Especially if you're a man, it's often hard to admit that you don't always have the answers. We don't even like to stop and ask for directions! Men are three and a half times more likely to commit suicide and I wonder if it's because we're expected to be strong and never ask for help. Without the help we need, we suffer in silence, and suffering in silence can lead to a depressing downward spiral. But whether you're a man or a woman, it's not only okay to ask for help, it's a requirement if you're going to live a productive, fulfilling life. You need the strength to be vulnerable.

Emotionally, things began looking a little more positive for me with the passage of time and my willingness to embrace my vulnerability in the face of my grief and pain. Financially, on the other hand, things were still a bit of a struggle in those days but they were definitely getting better. The company was growing. We were performing well and, as a result, our client base was getting larger. We were developing a good reputation. I worked hard in helping this all come about. I worked long hours interviewing, hiring, and training. The results showed. Our call center soon doubled in size and we moved to a larger location. My income rose and I was awarded with a bonus for my efforts.

Looking back, I credit much of my eventual success to my attitude. Even in the midst of my personal tragedies, somewhere down deep was a belief in myself and my future. I knew I could do the job. I had communication skills, I was determined, and I was committed to success. In the long run, I somehow knew that things were going to be okay. My attitude was what got me the job in the first place, after all, and I never stopped believing.

But success takes more than attitude. Much more. As it happens, if asking for help in one's personal life is a necessity, it's just as necessary in one's professional life. Attitude alone can't help you if you're doing things wrong or, for that matter, doing the wrong things. For personal support, you might, at certain times in your life, need the help of a therapist, or clergy person, or support group, or friends and family. For professional support, no matter who you are or what you think you know, you need something else, something more specific. Something that will provide you with the right start, even before you put your attitude or skills to work. For real career success, you need someone who's been where you're trying to go and who understands the challenges you're facing.

In a word, you need a mentor.

THREE

MENTORS: PATHWAYS TO SUCCESS

"Don't wish it were easier – wish you were better."

– JIM ROHN –

I was born with a competitive side. I've liked to compete—and win!—ever since I can remember. During the summers, from the age of ten to fifteen, I capitalized on that competitive side by joining my town's swim team. It was my first real experience in competitive sports and I loved every minute of it. One year, I was "Swimmer of the Year" for Pembroke, Massachusetts and I'm told my name is still displayed in the Pembroke Town Hall.

Swimming led to other competitive pursuits, including bodybuilding. I didn't set out to become a bodybuilder. I started lifting weights for high school football and for general development. But somewhere along the line, I met Dave Berman, a former football player, banker, and nationally competitive bodybuilder.

I took to Dave and Dave took to me. I wasn't necessarily looking for a mentor at the time, and, in fact, I'm pretty sure I didn't even know what a mentor was. But Dave became that to me. I began competing at the age of eighteen and would enter a total of six competitions. With Dave's help, I was successful. Second place would be my lowest finish. The highlights of my young career were winning my class in the 1984 Teenage Mr. USA held in Miami Beach, and placing second in the Teenage Mr. America competition in Worcester, Massachusetts that same year.

Here's the thing: I couldn't have done any of it without Dave. Dave taught me a lot about the technical aspects of bodybuilding. He taught me about training and diet. But he taught me more. Through example, Dave taught me about setting goals and "going for it." He taught me about the importance of discipline, dedication, and commitment, lessons I use to this day. With his own history in the sport (Dave had won countless trophies), he was an inspiration. I looked up to him and sought to emulate him. But Dave also managed to balance his hobby with his family and career. He taught me that, too. Overall, Dave became a fatherly figure to me.

It was a great lesson to learn at a relatively young age: people who have enjoyed success can teach others how to be successful, too. After all, those successful people probably learned their methods from other successful people before them. Most likely, anything you're considering doing has been done successfully before. That means there are people out there who have knowledge that you can use. People who can save you a lot of time and heartache.

> There are people out there who have knowledge that you can use. People who can save you a lot of time and heartache.

It's okay to want to forge your own path, but you'll get a much better start on where you're headed if you let someone else's experience help you navigate through challenges and obstacles that you might otherwise not even know exist until they trip you up. Why reinvent the wheel? In fact, if you stop and think about it, you probably started taking advantage of the experience of others as soon as you were born! If you're like most people, your very first mentors were your parents. Think of all that you learned from them over the years, good and bad. It's impossible to avoid the influence of those who raise you.

For me, I learned perspective and pragmatism from my mom. She was always able to put everything into its proper place. She taught me ethics and integrity, too. Her only real hates were lying and stealing. She caught me doing one of each of those as a child and her punishment (the belt) was all I needed for my lesson. My father was a hard worker and instilled in me a work ethic. He taught me manners, as well, and how to be kind, along with passing along the gift of gab. His favorite saying was, "It doesn't cost a thing to be nice." There was never a lot of overt affection on display in our house, but from both my parents, I learned love, compassion, and understanding.

You can probably think of especially influential teachers, too. I had several. Our lives are filled with mentors, especially when we're young. They're real time-savers. They can teach us in short order what it otherwise might take a long time to learn. When it came to bodybuilding, Dave Berman was certainly one of those people for me. Imagine if I had tried to learn bodybuilding on my own, with no real guidance or direction. No one to try to emulate or become inspired or motivated by. It might have taken years for me to get to the level I eventually reached. And by then, I wouldn't have been qualified for teen competitions anymore! Dave has since passed on, but during his time mentoring me, I enjoyed great camaraderie with others while training, and developed friendships that continue to this day. At the local gym, we were part of an interesting subculture of competitive bodybuilders, powerlifters, and football players, with several of us competing at the national level. Building these friendships was part of Dave's legacy, too.

In short, mentors are pathways to success. And I took this early lesson into the business world with me. My first real job was with a debt collection agency. Paul Leary, Sr., had built the business from scratch. He was the consummate hard-driving, self-made entrepreneur. As he interviewed me for the collector position I would take, he told me the qualities he was looking for in an employee. They were the same qualities that, collectively, he defined as the cornerstone of his company: dedication, commitment, and hard work.

Closing the interview, he issued a challenge that stuck with me. He said, "Eric, this company has performed extremely well. I'm proud of the many successes we've earned. We've taken on numerous large accounts, we've grown substantially, and we've become recognized as 'the best of the best' in the collection industry." I nodded approvingly. And then he said, "And we've done all of that without you. What are *you* going to do for us?"

I stopped nodding and stammered out some kind of answer, but it didn't really matter. Mr. Leary was intent on hiring me, anyway. He just wanted to lay down the challenge, giving me a preview of what I could expect from him and what he was expecting from me. He didn't want there to be any misunderstandings. "What are *you* going to do for us?" was a powerful question.

I went to work for Mr. Leary and closely observed his manner and studied the company he had built. In addition to being a terrific entrepreneur, Paul Leary was an amazing leader and motivator. Dave might have taught me the importance of goals, but Paul's goals were meteoric. He swung for the fences and rarely missed. He believed in himself and in his key people and his confidence was contagious. The clients that Paul typically landed were an impressive list and had complete faith when they placed their collection accounts with us.

With the employees, he was tough and demanding and he sometimes had a blunt way of talking. His manner intimidated some of the people who worked for him, but I sensed that Paul really knew what he was talking about. You could hear it in his sure and steady voice. I listened to him because I knew I could learn from him. I liked that he was demanding and I didn't care if he was blunt.

Besides, I noticed something about Paul's demanding nature. It worked. At least for me. Looking back, I can see that Paul was pushing me to excel in ways I probably wouldn't have thought I was ready for. He got more out of me than I would have thought possible. Yes, he was a task-master, but he could also inspire. You'd leave his office with a seemingly impossible list of marching orders, but at the same time, you'd leave feeling like a million bucks. He could do something that I've discovered is rare in people: he could make you believe in yourself.

I responded to Paul's management style and he responded to my work ethic. He pushed hard, and I welcomed it. Paul saw that I had the intangibles he'd been looking for. I was dedicated and committed. I had the right attitude; I had enthusiasm;

I relentlessly pursued our goals. Paul saw my potential long before I did. He saw in me what I didn't even know was there. He took extra time with me, guiding me and directing me. Under Paul's tutelage, I moved up quickly to a supervisory position. Within a year, just twenty-two years old, I was the manager of an entire department with four supervisors reporting to me.

Why did Paul invest so much time in me? I think it's because he knew I had some raw talent, but I also think it's because he saw that I wanted to gain the benefit of his experience and wisdom. I wanted to learn. I wanted to excel. That's the thing about a mentor. You typically don't have to look very hard for one. Mentors will find you. All you have to do is remain open, be coachable, teachable, and willing to learn and better yourself.

> To find a mentor, you have remain open, coachable, teachable, and willing to learn and better yourself.

Ultimately, Paul sold his business to a bigger organization. We both stayed on for a while. Eventually, Paul left, but before he did so, he ushered me into an office to tell me in private that he was leaving. Naturally, I was sorry to see him go. But he told me something in that office that day that has stayed with me my whole life. "Listen, Eric," he said, "you've got it. You'll always have it and don't let anybody ever tell you different." It was a tremendous boost and vote of confidence. From anyone else, it wouldn't have meant nearly as much. But from Paul Leary, it meant the world.

After Paul left the company, I reported to Peter Doolan. Peter had a different style altogether. But I've learned over the years that mentors come in a variety of flavors. Peter, for instance, was less intimidating than Paul, less blunt and a little more diplomatic. He was highly educated, with a master's degree or two. He taught me how to be more methodical. Peter was a numbers guy with an accounting background and had an approach that was less emotional and more calculated. This was especially good for me. Working with numbers wasn't my thing; the last math course I had passed was basic algebra in my freshman year of high school and I'm still not sure how I passed it. Peter taught me how to analyze and plan better. He taught me the importance of metrics and he taught me how to organize and execute. These are skills I would find to be invaluable later in my career.

In time, I left the debt collection company. After bouncing around here and there, I eventually saw an ad in a newspaper for selling self-improvement products by phone. For some reason, it caught my attention: "Inbound phone calls, full training," the ad read. Talk America was a full-service direct response marketing company of around 900 employees at the time that a man named Rob Graham founded. As the story goes, he'd started the company with a cash advance he'd taken on a credit card. Rob was highly creative, a real visionary.

I immediately took to the inbound-call/phone-sales job and within six months, won a sales contest that qualified me for a Caribbean cruise. Before long, I was part of an elite, top-selling phone team. I never worked for Rob directly, but I learned from him nevertheless. His creative vision rubbed off. The call center business would become my forte. And it wasn't just me that he influenced. I would guess at least twenty-five people who got their start with Rob went on to become entrepreneurs themselves, with several of them becoming millionaires. That's an amazing legacy, to set in motion that kind of opportunity for others.

A few of those guys began a start-up company called PowerTel. This is the new venture that lured me away from Talk America with an equity position. It was around the time of Jen and my mom's passing, and the partners of PowerTel were very helpful, supportive, and understanding. They all had solid and resourceful business minds, too, and during my time with them, I learned a lot.

Interestingly, my position with PowerTel was the first for which I was brought aboard because of my experience and know-how. Until then, I had started jobs at the most basic, entry-level positions. And therein lies a great lesson in learning. At both the debt-collection company and with call-center sales, I worked my way up the ladder with one major asset being my willingness to learn from those above me.

Why is this so important? Because it speaks to the idea that *anybody* can succeed if they have that same willingness, if they remain teachable and coachable. I had no special connections and I'm no genius. And it wasn't as if I had an MBA. I didn't have a business degree of any kind. In fact, I'd gone to the only college that would accept me, a local community one, but had dropped out in my second year. Higher education of the classroom variety wasn't for me. But what I learned from the people at those companies was enough to propel me to the top rungs.

And the people that I learned from, smart as they were, weren't magicians or miracle workers. They just happened to have the right knowledge, and that knowledge was replicable. It's as simple as that. *They provided opportunity and I took full advantage of it.*

The people that I learned from, smart as they were, weren't magicians or miracle workers. They just happened to have the right knowledge, and that knowledge was replicable.

While at PowerTel, following my personal tragedies, things eventually started getting better and my life began to turn around. And right around this time came, perhaps, the best mentor of my life: my brother. Steve is ten years older than me and he made a promise to our mother on her deathbed that he'd always look out for me. He's done that and more. Around the time of Mom's passing, Steve decided to leave the rat race he'd become a part of.

For years, Steve had been commuting an hour and fifteen minutes each way to his job as the chief operating officer of a publicly held technology company. He'd had enough of the corporate world and decided to start his own company, a call center, as a matter of fact. The company, Triton Technologies, Inc., would be in Massachusetts. With or without me, he was going to forge ahead, but he knew that my experience could prove valuable to the new venture and he invited me in as a partner.

To get the business going, we needed to secure a line of credit. Of course, I had filed that bankruptcy not long before. Credit certainly wasn't anything I had access to. Not only did Steve bring me into the business, he also signed for my portion of the line of credit. Going a step further, with me moving down from Maine, he even invited me to live with him and his wife and family until I could get on my feet and get my own place.

Steve was the new company's CEO and his strength was that he was an operational genius. He had knowledge and experience, along with a remarkable ability to anticipate and solve problems. My strength was experience in training and inside sales within the call center environment. We worked well together with a third partner, our CFO Andy Bank. It was obviously a big step for me, to build and manage a call center for a business that I had a partnership stake in. Steve showed confidence in me and that confidence was invaluable. From Steve, I learned the importance of operational excellence. With his business acumen and experience, he established a corporate culture that gave everybody something to live up to. He was a true leader. To me, Steve was not only a mentor and brother, but a best friend. He still is.

I've had plenty of other mentors in my life. Truthfully, there are too many mentors to give proper credit to. It seems that at every stage of my life, a mentor came along. The point should be clear: you can learn from anyone. The only condition? You have to be *willing* to learn. Just like asking for help with major life issues, this willingness often requires some humility, an open admittance to yourself that you don't have all the answers. The key is to find the people who do.

Finding a mentor isn't that hard if you're truly interested in learning. If you're interested in learning, you can't help but stumble upon people who are in your field that know more than you know. Ask them for help. Ask them questions. You can even ask them if they'd like to be your mentor, although the relationship doesn't really need to be that formal. Sometimes, just hanging around such a person is enough to enable you to soak in their knowledge.

Collectively, my mentors taught me communication skills, goal-setting, motivation, leadership, entrepreneurship, and a host of other skills. In return, I listened to them and showed them the intangible qualities that drew them toward me in the first place. I only had to bring to the table a couple of essential prerequisites: a winning attitude and a high level of enthusiasm. And that's all it took to form the mentor/mentee relationship.

> Deciding you need a mentor requires some humility, an open admittance to yourself that you don't have all the answers. And to know that the key is to find the people who do.

For a while, I often wondered how I could pay these hugely instrumental people back. Of course, I like to think my performance for them made us even, but, in truth, I know that in the long run, I probably got more out of these relationships than they did. Finally, I came upon the best way for anybody to pay back a mentor: by paying it forward. By becoming a mentor yourself. What a wonderful way to keep the cycle moving.

The best way you can pay back a mentor is to pay it forward. Be a mentor yourself!

I'm proud to say I've mentored dozens of people, some of whom have gone on to be great successes. In doing so, I've learned that being a mentor is its own reward. It's enormously gratifying to see someone blossoming under your guidance. If you've experienced success and have yet to share the knowledge you've gained along the way, I implore you to find someone out there who needs a leg up. You'll be glad you did. Until then, keep learning yourself. There are people in this world who have knowledge you can use. All you have to do is ask. And then listen.

FOUR

THE INTANGIBLES

*"Soft skills get little respect
but they will make or break your career."*

– Peggy Klaus, author –

We talked in the last chapter about the idea of being coachable and teachable and willing to learn. These attributes come under a more general umbrella that I would refer to simply as "attitude." With the right attitude, you can overcome whatever your obstacles to success might be.

Everyone generally agrees with this, of course. It's pretty much understood that a winning attitude is a prerequisite for success. But let's look at this question of attitude a little deeper. Let's really examine it. What does it mean to have a "winning attitude"? What characteristics are necessary? How, on an everyday basis, does one need to act? What does a winning attitude *look like*?

When my son Alex was in middle school, he began to experience some academic challenges. In particular, he had some issues with math word problems. He could do math computations, but if the math problem was structured as a word problem, he had trouble with it. A simple equation he could solve. A math problem written out in the form of a paragraph, on the other hand, presented a real difficulty. It would throw him for a loop. Unlike a simple equation, with a word problem, it was as if there was too much information for Alex to make sense of.

Through testing by a pediatric neuropsychologist, it was determined that Alex suffered from executive functioning disorder (EFD). EFD often comes hand in hand with attention deficit disorder. With executive functioning disorder, you have trouble with higher-level tasks such as planning, analyzing, and organizing. It's often hard to complete projects or even know where to start. After the diagnosis, we put Alex in a school with other mainstream students who also had learning differences (EFD, ADD, and dyslexia). Alex thrived in that environment, with smaller class sizes and strong support tools. The school was the answer to our prayers. Through middle school and now high school, Alex is earning A's and B's. So far, so good.

But here's the thing: in the course of learning about Alex's EFD, I discovered something. Although nobody really knows the cause, there's enough research to suggest the condition might be passed from parent to child. There may very well be a genetic connection to such a learning disability. And when I discovered this, a light bulb went on. Alex's difficulties seemed eerily familiar to me. I, too, had problems with analysis, organization, planning, even concentrating. After Alex's testing, I had testing done, too. The result? No surprise: I had the same executive functioning deficits, along with evidence of inattentive ADD.

That explained why my academic career hadn't exactly been stellar. I graduated from high school, but just barely. It also explained how, even as an adult, I often struggled with things that seemed easy for others. Staying organized was always a challenge for me. If I had several tasks before me, I'd find myself feeling overwhelmed by anxiety, not knowing where or how to start. It would be as if I'd become paralyzed, unsure of what to do first. I would notice other people rolling along, multitasking and I would always wonder how that could even be possible.

In thinking about this, I wondered how it was, then, that I had managed to make a success of myself. I'd had no access to the kind of programs Alex had. Back when I was his age, we never heard of learning disabilities. In school, more than once, I was told my problem was that I wasn't "applying" myself. Time and again, a teacher would tell me, "Eric, you just need to apply yourself," as if there was some kind of magical "apply" switch I could flip and suddenly I'd start getting high marks. People would have scoffed at the idea of a learning disability.

And yet, I had been a successful swimmer and a successful bodybuilder. I played football in high school, too, and I was pretty good at it. But there was a difference. A big difference. I cared about those things. I could focus on them. There was a competitive angle to them that somehow caused me to exceed even my own expectations. Then again, my expectations were high. I believed in myself. And so I became committed and dedicated. I worked hard. With just a little success, I found myself feeling a level of enthusiasm that made me even more committed. In short, when it came to these pursuits, I had *a winning, can-do attitude.*

I took that attitude with me into the business world and met with success. And that's what a winning attitude looks like. It's not just positive thinking (although that never hurts). It's more than that. It's all of those little characteristics, like commitment and dedication and enthusiasm and hard work that, collectively, allow one to be able to overcome the biggest obstacles.

A winning attitude is not just positive thinking. It's more than that. It's all of those little characteristics, like commitment and dedication and enthusiasm and hard work.

Keep in mind that when I was enjoying my successes, I didn't even know I had the obstacle of a learning disability. Had I known, I might have been able to find an effective workaround that might have made my life a lot easier. But that just goes to show what the effect of attitude can be. I pushed through the obstacle with nothing to guide me or help me. Just my attitude. And my attitude served me well when I came upon other obstacles, ones I knew were there, like the ones I detailed in Chapter 1.

Let's talk about competitiveness, a key component of a winning attitude. When I interviewed for the debt collection job with Paul Leary, he looked at my background and liked the bodybuilding experience. He believed that my competitive fire in that pursuit could be harnessed for the job he was offering me. If I was competitive in one thing, I could be competitive in another. Paul was right. In the interview, Paul told me, among other things, that he was looking for the kind of employee who would show up to work early and leave late. That turned out to be me, and not just because I was hoping to impress the boss. I showed up early and stayed late because I wanted the extra time. I felt as if it gave me an edge and I was always looking for an edge. I wanted to be the best.

That competitive drive is what allowed me to focus. If you're focused, you can overcome whatever is standing in your way. Focus allows you to concentrate all of your efforts on the task at hand. Had I been able to focus on my grades in high school ("apply" myself, as the teachers said), I could have done much, much better. But, you see, I didn't have the competitive drive for grades. It just wasn't there and I couldn't conjure it up. Swimming, bodybuilding, and other physical activities? You bet. Classroom work? Nope.

There's a lesson here: if you're doing something that you just can't get yourself excited about, no matter how hard you try, then you probably need to start thinking about another pursuit. It's impossible to manufacture competitive fire out of thin air. You have it or you don't. You can't fool your brain, not for very long, anyway. Find something that excites you and you'll feel an inherent desire to succeed at it. You'll find yourself *focused* on it. Obstacles that seemed insurmountable, will suddenly seem easy, or at least manageable.

It's impossible to manufacture competitive fire out of thin air. If you're doing something that you just can't get yourself excited about, then you need to find another pursuit.

When you're focused, you're confident. You don't have time to harbor doubts or wonder if you're good enough. You just do whatever needs doing. Focused people, therefore, typically appear to have strong and healthy egos. They carry themselves with an air of quiet, calm urgency. But remember what we learned in the last chapter. A healthy ego is a fine thing, but it helps to maintain a little humility, too. You don't, and can't, know everything. Be strong enough to know when you need to ask for help. That takes confidence, too. Think of confidence and humility as being two sides of the same coin.

Here's an example. When Alex was three years old, we signed him up for karate classes. We knew karate would be a great way to teach him discipline and the rewards of hard work. Watching Alex in his karate class inspired me to try the adult karate class. It looked like a fun challenge. My kind of thing. And I'd always respected people who had earned their black belt. I knew what a black belt represented and it was always in the back of my mind to earn one myself. It turned out that this style of karate at the adult level was particularly demanding in every sense of the word. This was fine by me. I wanted to push myself to the limit. And I had the confidence to do it. I knew that if I set my mind to it, I could get that belt.

In the initial class, one of the first things my master instructor said was this: check your ego at the door. There was no room in his class for anybody who wasn't serious enough about the instructor's particular brand of martial arts to follow his instructions to the letter. This wasn't a creative writing course or an art seminar. The instructor had a very exacting methodology that required the students to pay strict attention. And, in fact, the students who did the best were the ones who came into this instructor's class with no preconceived ideas as to how to proceed. They listened to him. They knew he had the knowledge. They had the *humility* necessary to learn. And the confidence to allow themselves to be humble.

Successful people have the humility necessary to learn. And the confidence to allow themselves to be humble.

Confidence and humility. See how they work together? Don't let your ego get in the way of your confidence. Oh, and by the way, it took four years of dedication, but I got that black belt. In fact, I went on to survive a total of three black belt tests—some of the toughest but most rewarding challenges of my life.

All of these things—your competitiveness and focus, your ability to check your ego, your confidence and humility—along with your enthusiasm, commitment, dedication, and hard work are all attitudinal characteristics that I like to refer to as *the intangibles*. They can't really be measured, in other words. After all, how can you measure competitiveness? How can you measure one's desire to succeed? Is there a scale for dedication? And yet, as unquantifiable as these factors are, they're also very necessary prerequisites to success. Throughout my career, these intangibles, or "soft skills," were high on a shortlist of things that I could bring to the party.

Although you can't measure someone's desire to succeed, you can certainly tell when it's missing. There is no hiding the results of someone's performance who has these intangibles in short supply. The halls of mediocrity are filled with people whose level of focus and drive is low or average. You can tell the people who come to work not a minute before they have to and who stampede out the door precisely at 5:00 p.m. You can tell by their level of success, or, perhaps, I should say their lack of success. The proverbial bottom line is ruthless.

Conversely, you can tell the people who have the intangibles in abundance. Their results are anything but intangible. Bank account balances, assets, investments—these are all measurable. Interesting, isn't it? *Tangible results come from intangible qualities.*

Tangible results come from intangible qualities.

Now, here's a question I get asked a lot: can you learn the intangibles? Personally, I don't think so. You either have the drive to succeed or you don't. You're either a competitive person or you're not. However, with that said, let's remember my example about my grades in school versus my bodybuilding and swimming. It's not that I wasn't a competitive person in high school; it's that I wasn't a competitive person with respect to classroom work. I suspect that if you're reading this book, you have the drive to succeed. I can't impart that to you, but if you're taking the time to read this, I don't have to. You have some level of drive to better yourself or you wouldn't have picked up a book like this one in the first place. You've got the intangibles that you need. If you're stuck in life, the problem might be that your intangibles are not being utilized in the proper direction.

If you're stuck, check your level of motivation.

So if I can't impart upon you the intangibles, I can at least suggest that you check your level of motivation. What excites you? What gets you up in the morning? What makes you want to work overtime and hardly even consider it work? There's no right or wrong answer. Some people are motivated by money. If that's you, then fine. At least as a primary source of motivation, money has never really worked for me. Paul Leary used to say, "Bigger paychecks, bigger headaches." I've learned that he was right! Money's a great way to keep score and measure your success. And sure, it can provide you with more options in life. But, in and of itself, money won't buy you happiness.

Me, I've always been motivated more by recognition and appreciation, which are great ways to have your success measured by your peers, clients, and other industry insiders who notice your accomplishments and know what it took. Other people are motivated by the work itself. A painter might want to paint simply because she loves the creative act of painting. Some people are motivated not by the work, but by the results—the good things that the work might bring about, for themselves or others.

The point is, you need to find what drives *you.* The intangibles are there, just waiting to be accessed and put into gear. If you do what you love to do, there's not a whole lot that's going to be able to stop you.

FIVE

TREATING OTHERS WELL:
THE BEST INVESTMENT YOU CAN MAKE IN YOURSELF

"Respect is how to treat everyone."

– RICHARD BRANSON –

You'd think a chapter on treating others well would be a pretty short chapter. It's common sense, right? It's automatic. It's everybody's default mode. Well, not exactly. The evidence seems to suggest otherwise. We've all experienced it: you call a customer service number with a problem and you get treated not like a valued customer, but like an interruption in the day of the person handling your call. You can almost see their eyes rolling. Or the clerk at the counter of the deli you stop into for lunch looks like he'd rather be anywhere than behind that counter. And he confirms your suspicion with the gruff tone of his voice and the lack of a simple smile.

There seems to be general agreement these days that customer service is not what it used to be. We're often treated indifferently and, sometimes, even rudely. But I would submit that the problem goes deeper than just customer service. Indifference and rudeness are not confined to the world of commerce. They're a societal phenomenon.

The same lack of simple politeness and care that we see too often in the business world is evident everywhere we go. We see it in the supermarket from the person in the "ten items or less" lane with a cart overloaded with groceries, to the person in traffic who's in too big a hurry to be bothered with simple courtesies like using a turning signal or, God forbid, letting someone merge in front of him in heavy traffic. And how many times have you allowed someone to merge in front of you and not received a simple wave or nod of thanks in return? I'm sure you probably have your own examples and you probably don't have to go back in time very far. This morning? Yesterday?

When did we get this way? I'm sure there are all manner of theories. Mine is that our digital world has created two inherent problems. First, technology has speeded things up to the point where we all expect things to happen *now*. Expect? We *demand* things now. Are you old enough to remember the days when you would order something and were told to expect "four to six weeks for delivery"? Can you imagine this today? Don't get me wrong. I love the convenience of ordering something and having it show up the next day. But with this convenience, I'm afraid we've all lost the ability to be patient. We don't know how to wait. We're all running at the speed of light, cursing whoever dares get in our way.

> These days, it seems we're all out of touch with our fellow world travelers and, consequently, we're out of practice in dealing with them.

Second, we spend so much time looking at our computer screens or smartphones that we've forgotten how to interact with our fellow human beings. Our entry into the digital world has meant we've unwittingly separated ourselves off from the real world of flesh and blood and genuine human feelings. We're out of touch with our fellow world travelers and, consequently, we're out of practice in dealing with them. We've forgotten how to relate to people on a personal level. Our communications take place in emails and texts to people we might never have even met face to face!

Maybe I've noticed it more because courtesy and manners and being polite were drilled into me as a child. Both my parents emphasized these simple things, my father especially, with his favorite saying, "It doesn't cost you anything to be nice." It was a wonderful piece of advice that I've always carried with me. We moved when I was nine and I remember the teachers in my new school remarking to my mother, "My goodness, your son is so well-mannered!"

It doesn't cost you anything to be nice!

The thing is, my inclination to be nice to people has paid off for me in the business world. But that's not why I'm nice to people. I'm nice to people because it's right to be nice to people. Plain and simple. I treat people the way I'd like to be treated. The Golden Rule, "Do unto others as you would have them do unto you," is a maxim that, in one form or another, you'll find in pretty much every religion on earth and it goes back thousands of years. And yet, we still seem to have trouble following it.

It's hard to believe that it's so difficult to abide by such a simple, logical guideline. My dad was right. It doesn't cost anything to hold the door open for somebody, or to drive courteously (which is also safer!), or to say "please" and "thank you" or "you're welcome." And what I've noticed is that these gestures are almost always met in kind. People respond to courteousness, in other words. (Maybe because it's getting so rare!) If I smile at someone, it's not often that I don't get a smile returned to me. Then we both feel a little bit better about the world. The days of two people get just a little brighter now. And to think, the whole transaction didn't cost a thing.

Some people think that smiling if you're not in the mood to smile makes you a phony. But the truth is, a smile can actually put you in a good mood. Science bears this out. So don't wait for a good mood to smile. Smile and allow the good mood to follow! Most importantly, your smile might just touch off a good mood in someone else. Then they'll smile to somebody and brighten that person's day. And on it goes.

Don't wait for a good mood to smile. Smile and allow the good mood to follow!

That's not always the case, of course. I may smile and say, "Thank you," to that guy behind the deli counter when he hands me my order and I might get back nothing but a grunt. And have you noticed these days how many places like this now have tip jars? It's as though a tip is obligatory now for counter service, even with little or no promise of courtesy or appreciation in return. When did that start? Nevertheless, I'm still going to smile and say, "Thank you." I might even tip. If I get a grunt back, I get a grunt back. I'm not going to allow that to stop me from going forth in the world acting kindly toward other people. I won't let a grunt bring me down.

It's not that I think people today are inherently *un*kind. I don't think people leave their homes in the morning with the idea that they're going to purposely behave in discourteous ways. Nobody uses bad manners intentionally. In fact, I'd bet that if you polled random people on the street, close to one-hundred percent would tell you that they are well-mannered, courteous, and considerate of their fellow human beings. We all like to think that about ourselves, right? But, of course, that's not what we see in our everyday lives. Our experiences tell us the number of well-mannered and courteous people is far, far below one-hundred percent.

Why the disconnect? I think it's a matter of awareness. If you've been reading this chapter and nodding along, agreeing with my assessment of today's state of affairs, and thinking the problem is *other* people, you might not realize that, at times, you could be part of the problem. How aware are you of your own behavior? I'll admit to my glaring imperfections if you'll admit to yours. We've all had those days. We're down, we're depressed, we're in a hurry, we're stressed out, we're running behind—whatever the reason, it all adds up to the same thing: we're in our own little world, focused inwardly instead of outwardly. We're just not *aware* of our fellow human beings and, further, we're not aware of our own behaviors toward them. It's nothing intentional. We're just lost inside ourselves.

Often what happens is that when we focus inward and think in terms of me, me, me, we start to believe that somehow our agenda is much more important than the next person's. Our plate is more full than their plate. The problems we're challenged with are more significant than the problems they're challenged with. Our time is more valuable. Subconsciously, we begin to believe that we have a right to be in a rush, to be short with people, to remain unaware of our effect on others, even to be impolite. We proceed along as if the problem is that other people just don't understand our unique problems and worries and stresses.

In time, this line of thinking becomes a self-fulfilling prophecy. Eventually, you end up alienating everyone around you and then you really *do* have serious problems to face!

From time to time, we could all use a moment to look in the mirror and see if we're the kind of people we want to be. Because here's the thing: if you act poorly in your everyday life, you're going to act poorly in your work life, too. I don't care how great a salesperson you are, if you're in the habit of bad manners, you're not going to be able to throw a switch during working hours and suddenly become likable—the kind of person others want to do business with. Instead, you're going to carry your behavior into your work world with you. It's inescapable.

> How aware are you of your own behavior? From time to time, we could all use a moment to look in the mirror and see if we're the kind of people we want to be.

You know what one of my secrets was when I first started in the call center business? I smiled into the phone when I took my calls. Sounds silly, doesn't it? This wasn't Skype or Facetime, after all. These were just regular phone connections where one party had no idea what the other party looked like, let alone what their expression was. Nevertheless, the first line in our phone script was always: *Smile.* I learned quickly that people can "see" a smile in your tone of voice. We were even told that if we needed to use a mirror to remind ourselves to smile, we should do so.

That idea about the mirror is a good one, and not just for your smile. Think of the mirror as a metaphor for looking at your actions and taking an honest self-inventory. Think about how you related to others today. Were you courteous? Did you treat the other person with kindness? Compassion? Did you remember to smile? In your everyday interactions with people, are you using the basic manners we were all taught as children? Always say "excuse me" and "please" and "may I." Remember that a thank you is followed by "you're welcome," rather than just "have a good one," or, worse, a grunt!

Kindness also means respect and respect often involves reciprocity. Many times in my career, I showed support or encouragement to someone who was down, or congratulated someone for some milestone or achievement. Most of the time, these very same people responded in kind when I was down, or when I achieved something. But at other times, some of these people were nowhere to be found. Nobody owes you anything, of course, and you have no right to demand a reciprocal exchange of concern or well-wishing. But it's always a good idea to remember when someone has gone out of their way to recognize you in some way so that you can do the same for them. Hopefully, it'll be returned. It's a matter of respect and respect is a matter of kindness. Richard Branson said it best: "Respect is how to treat everyone."

Here's the good news about today's relative decline in polite behavior and good manners: if you start paying attention to how *you're* coming across to others and how *you're* really treating them, you're going to have a big advantage over your competition. Whatever the industry or line of work, all things being equal, the smiling, friendly, courteous, kind person is going to have a big edge over the unsmiling, unfriendly, discourteous, unkind person.

Simply put, people want to do business with people they like. Often, they're even willing to pay a premium for it. You've probably experienced it yourself. You'll bypass a restaurant with terrific food because you can't stand the service. You'll go somewhere else and pay more money for food that might not even be as good, but where you know they'll welcome your presence and treat you like royalty. It doesn't matter what your product or service is, if you can separate yourself from your competition with courteousness and professionalism, you'll have all the advantage you'll need.

> If you can separate yourself from your competition with courteousness and professionalism, you'll have all the advantage you'll need.

Here's an example right out of my everyday life. I go to the same donut shop in the next town for coffee every day and often twice a day. Why go out of my way, when I can make coffee at home or go to a shop that's closer and more convenient? Because from the owner to the managers of this shop, to each employee, everyone treats me special. And, of course, it's not just me. I've noticed the way they treat every customer. They make sure to get your order correct every time and they do it with a smile. It seems to be embedded in the company DNA. It's clear that every new hire meets the owner's exceptional service standard. No doubt the owner, a sharp, hardworking entrepreneur, has discovered that in such a competitive space, his philosophy to set his shop apart with excellent service pays off.

This same philosophy is shared by the gentleman who cuts my hair. He charges a premium, but it's in return for the absolute best in quality and service. Rocco always checks in with me afterward to be sure I'm happy. He's ultra-accommodating when it comes to scheduling appointments. And, again, it's not just me. This is his approach with every customer. Some who work for Rocco at his salon refer to him as old-school. Well, old-school works. Rocco has clients who have been coming to him for ten, twenty, and even thirty-plus years. He more than earns the premium that he charges.

Choosing to do business with people we like and who treat us well is simply human nature and we're now back to the Golden Rule. Using the Golden Rule in business invokes an ethical philosophy known as "enlightened self-interest." Essentially, this means that if you act in such a way so as to further the aims of others, you'll ultimately further your own aims. It's a simple philosophy and a true one. Master motivator Zig Ziglar put it like this: "You will get all you want in life if you just help enough other people get what they want." It all starts with understanding and empathy. It all starts with treating others the way you'd want to be treated, by making, as your default mode, "being nice" and performing acts of kindness. It's simple, yet foolproof.

Here's something else that's interesting: I've found that you can get ahead with this philosophy *even with your competitors*. Over my career, I became good friends with many a competitor. When it gets right down to it, it's typically a pretty small world within any given industry. You bump into the same people over and over again and a lot of those same people are competing against you. But that should never mean you treat them any worse than you would treat anybody else. These people aren't natural enemies. They're people just like you trying to make a living. In fact, maybe you should treat them even better than anybody else. "Keep your friends close," goes the old saying. "Keep your enemies closer."

The fact is, unless you're in a dying industry (in which case, you should get out), there's always enough business to go around. Your competitors face the same struggles and the same problems as you do. If you ever sat down with them and shared ideas, you might be surprised at what you have in common, not to mention what you could learn from them.

And be thankful they're there. Competition only makes you better. I learned this long ago in my swimming career. It's no coincidence that some of the greatest rivals in sports went on to become such great friends. Basketball's Magic Johnson and Larry Bird is one example. Tennis's Chris Evert and Martina Navratilova is another. Sure, there were times when they might have hated each other, but they always respected each other, and when the dust settled, they developed close friendships.

Plus, people often change companies. Your competitor today might be working with you tomorrow. This is exactly what happened to me. A top leader at one of Triton's fiercest competitors eventually came to work for me and became an invaluable part of our operation. He brought a lot of knowledge and experience and his competitive fire was a huge asset once he started using it for us and not the competition! The best part might have been that he became a good friend. Would that have happened if I had taken a cut-throat approach and treated him ruthlessly while he had competed against us? Probably not.

Whether it's your competitors, customers, suppliers, or the people you come across in the normal course of your day, remember my father's advice. After all, I can't imagine a better investment you could make in yourself. Being kind to others: it doesn't cost a thing and the upside is enormous. Where else can you get that kind of return?

SIX

COMMUNICATION:
THE FOUNDATION OF EVERYTHING PEOPLE RELATED

*"The most important thing in communication
is hearing what isn't said."*

— PETER DRUCKER —

When CEOs are asked what they look for in employees, especially top-level employees, one thing routinely stands out. This attribute is often considered more important than education, knowledge, or experience. The magic quality? Interpersonal communication skills. Warren Buffet once said, "The one way to become worth fifty percent more than you are now—at least—is to hone your communication skills, both written and verbal."

The ability to effectively communicate is not an option for anyone seriously engaged in furthering their career. If you're stagnating, or not getting where you want to go quickly enough, have you considered the way in which you interact with others? This may take some serious introspection and brutal self-honesty. But it's worth it. More than anything else, your failure to properly connect with people in your professional life could well be holding you back.

> The ability to effectively communicate is not an option for anyone seriously engaged in furthering their career.

Communication is the foundation of everything "people-related." And it's much more than just knowing what to say. It's also knowing *how* and even *when*. These days, communication can take many forms. Each form is important in its own way and each form has its own place.

The most intimate and, therefore, the form with the most potential (for good or for bad), is face to face. A one-on-one meeting with someone in their home or office or, say, over a cup of coffee at a restaurant, can set you up for a positive, successful outcome. It can also set you up for failure, depending on what kind of impression you make. Such is the power of the face-to-face.

From the face-to-face meeting, the forms of communication begin to degrade in effectiveness, increasing the chances of misunderstandings or confusion. This starts with the less personal group situation and runs downward to telephone conversations (or maybe Skype or Facetime), and then to written correspondence including, in order of decreasing potential value, letters, emails, social media communications, and, finally, the text message, where, these days, we often say what we want to say with a smiley-face emoticon or thumbs-up symbol.

One big advantage of face-to-face communication over other forms of communication is that it gives you nonverbal clues. You can judge by a person's facial expression or posture what he or she is thinking. If she's furrowing her brow, maybe she's confused. If her arms are crossed and she appears standoffish, maybe she's skeptical. If you're droning on and on about something and you see the person you're talking to repeatedly checking her phone, or yawning, you might want to stop droning. You won't get this opportunity with a too-long email that you've written. You won't be able to see that the recipient read the first two sentences and then went back to his inbox to look for something more interesting.

In person, through expressions and body language, you're able to read boredom, interest, amusement, anger, sympathy, rejection, approval, skepticism, frustration, surprise, or any number of emotions that the person might not be conveying with words alone. It's a form of language all its own. These non-verbal clues can't be overestimated.

Take this example of a conversation, first taking place face-to-face, then taking place through text messaging:

Face-to-Face:

Joyce: "John, it would really help me out if I could have your report on my desk by the end of this week."

John, smiling and nodding, relieved that Joyce doesn't need it earlier: "Fine!"

Joyce: "Great!"

Text:

Joyce, pulling out her phone, late for a meeting and wanting to dash off a quick text: "Need report by end of week!"

John, several long minutes later: "Fine."

Joyce, to herself: "Uh-oh. What does 'fine' mean? Is that sarcasm??"

Joyce might be right about the sarcasm, but we'll never really know. Can *you* tell by John's answer? It's curt, but then again, it's a text message which are generally shorter by design. He took his time returning it, so was he collecting himself so he didn't reply angrily? Or was he in the middle of something else and just didn't have a chance to reply right away? He might be upset by the deadline, he might be upset by the demanding nature of the text, or he might not be upset at all and really meant that he finds the request "fine." Pleased with the assignment's time limit, or reacting passive-aggressively to it, only John knows for sure.

For Joyce, the matter has become one of interpretation, which is fraught with opportunities for misunderstanding. Is John not happy with his work? Should she start looking for his replacement? John has to interpret, too. Notwithstanding the deadline, which may or may not be acceptable, was Joyce out of line with the demanding nature of the texted request? What if he knew she was in a hurry and most likely didn't mean to be so blunt? But, of course, from a distance, he had no way to know. He can only guess. He might wonder why she was demanding. Is she unhappy with his work? Should he start looking for another job? (Hopefully, these two sit down together soon and clear the air!)

It's important to remember, however, that as effective as face-to-face interaction can be, sometimes it's just not possible. Sometimes, emailing or texting might be all you have at your disposal. No form of communication is necessarily bad. If the person you're communicating with prefers text messaging, then you need to be fluent in it. Communication is all about *connecting,* and forcing a phone call on a person who'd prefer an email or text message is a sure way to undermine your own efforts. The key is to think it through. Joyce should have taken more time, and it wouldn't have taken much to clarify her position. She could have easily softened her request by adding a "please" or even a smiley face, both of which might have taken two more seconds and alleviated a lot of potential angst.

In other words, the lessons from Chapter 5 apply entirely to communication, and to all forms of it. Remember basic courteousness and manners. In sending a text, think about the text *you'd* like to receive. Think about the tone of it and the wording of it. Remember the magic words of "please" and "thank you." And remember, too, that "please" is spelled p-l-e-a-s-e, not "pls." "Thank you" is t-h-a-n-k y-o-u, not "ty." If you can't take the time to type in the extra letters, how sincere will your recipient think you are? Especially in the business world, formal is better than informal. Use your abbreviations and slang sparingly, if at all.

The most important part of communication, and yet the most overlooked part, might surprise you. It's surprising because we don't think of it as a means of expression, but it certainly is. Can you guess what it is? If you said *listening*, give yourself a pat on the back.

The most important part of communication—listening— is the most overlooked.

Often times, it's so important for us to *tell* people what we want to say, that we don't pay attention to what they want to tell *us*. And yet, without knowing what, specifically, they want to talk about, or what's important to them regarding the given subject matter of the conversation, how can you know what to say? How can you know what will resonate with them? How can you know that everything you're talking about won't simply go in one ear and out the other?

Have you ever been stuck next to someone on a plane who just couldn't stop talking? Or cornered at a social gathering by a person who felt the need to go on and on about him or herself? You know the type. They're not interested in communicating, they're interested in talking. The difference is easy to spot. The talker never asks questions, never asks you about you. Never stops talking! They end up conducting a continual monologue rather than engaging in two-way dialogue.

The communicator, on the other hand, engages with you, asks curious questions, listens to you and pays attention. The communicator responds to what you're saying. The communicator expresses interest in you. He or she clearly cares about you. *That's* what gets expressed by good listening.

Good listening requires being fully present. I don't mean physically, which, as we've said, is preferable. I mean being present mentally, even if you're not in the same room. Even if you're not in the same state or even country. It means being focused on the conversation, on what's being said, and in what tone of voice. It means not allowing your mind to wander. We've all had the experience of talking to someone and watching as they nod along, seemingly picking up on every word, only to have them ask a question that betrays the fact that they weren't really listening at all! They'll ask something you just answered a minute before.

This happens all the time. If you're honest, you know that you've been that person, too. I know I have. People talk to us and we pretend to listen—and might even believe that we are!—but in reality, we're thinking about our weekend or where we're going to go for lunch. In other words, we aren't listening. We're not present. And many times, we're thinking about what *we're* going to say next, rather than listening to what the other person is saying right now. Listening demands attention and focus.

Our ability to communicate is so vitally important because it's one of the main things that people judge us by, and certainly one of the first. We make an immediate impression based on how we say hello, or shake someone's hand, or how we word the very first sentence in an introductory email. If you blow it on the first impression, it's often hard to get an opportunity to make a second. Your first impression—your first communication—is what will be remembered. Success in almost every people-intensive endeavor is related directly to our ability to effectively communicate.

Speaking skills are important, but so are writing skills. You don't need to be Shakespeare, but there's no excuse for sending correspondence with misspellings and grammatical errors. Do you know when to use "there" versus "their" versus "they're"? Do you know the difference between "to" and "too" and "two"? "Your" and "you're"? Do you know the basics of punctuation? Not long ago, I saw a sign outside of a restaurant that advertised fresh fish and it was written like so: "Fresh" fish. Now, I assume they wanted to emphasize the "fresh" part, but instead of underlining it or maybe making it bold, they put quotation marks around it, thus making me wonder if it was really fresh or just "fresh."

> Our ability to communicate is so vitally important because it's one of the main things that people judge us by, and certainly one of the first.

I've received solicitation letters from companies seeking my business that were riddled with errors. I've even received letters where my name was misspelled! Is there ever an excuse for this kind of sloppiness? If the company didn't take the time to have their letter proofread, or to determine the correct spelling of my name, why would I think they'll care about doing a good job for me with whatever it is they're trying to sell me? Spelling is basic. Can I trust a company or an individual that doesn't pay attention to the basics?

As with the principles in the last chapter, much of this requires an honest self-evaluation. There's no shame in admitting that you might need some help in certain areas. We all do. How is your command of the English language? Could you stand a little improvement with your vocabulary or your knowledge of the rules of grammar? What about your speaking ability? Can you properly articulate your points? Are you always clearly heard and understood? Are you comfortable and secure with being able to communicate with different people? One on one? In group situations?

Look around for adult education courses. Take some business writing courses or enroll in some speaking classes. Join Toastmasters. Or find a private coach to work on all of this with you. You don't have to have an MBA in speech or a degree in English. But you do need to be competent in the manner in which you communicate with others. And the more competent you are, the better an impression you'll make.

The good news here is that these skills are learnable. Nobody is born as a great communicator. The best communicators in history—whether writers like William Shakespeare, Charles Dickens, or Ernest Hemingway, or speakers like Abraham Lincoln, Winston Churchill, or Martin Luther King, Jr.—all started at the same place we all start—unable to utter or write a single coherent word!

> Nobody is born as a great communicator. The good news is that communication skills are learnable!

You might want to seek help to improve your communication skills if:

1 You communicate regularly with someone of importance (a boss, a client, or even your spouse!),

2 You simply want to speak better in your day-to-day dealings with people,

3 You want to be able to state your position with the right impact,

4 You find yourself sometimes needing to deliver tough news and you'd like to be able to do so with the best positive spin,

5 You want to develop your number one communication tool: Listening!

Here's one huge communication skill that you don't need a class to learn: *responsiveness*. This might be the easiest, and yet most neglected, skill of all. It's so simple it defies reason as to why it's so often overlooked. Someone calls, you call them back. Promptly. Someone emails you, you email them back. Promptly. You *respond*. How simple can it be! And yet, we've all experienced the opposite of this. You call a plumbing company because your sink is backed up, leave a voicemail because nobody is apparently in the office, and you never hear back. You walk into a store with money to spend and nobody's around to help you. You shoot an email to a printer asking for a quote on some sales material and you get an email back—a week later!

This skill is becoming even more important in our digital world. We all have smartphones and email accounts. We all know when someone is trying to get in touch with us. We can't pretend we didn't see a text or didn't know that someone left a voicemail. So, even if you can't get to it today, you'd better let them know you've seen it today. Sometimes all it takes is a simple, "Received your email! I can help. Will respond in more detail first thing in the a.m.!" Most people are respectful of someone else's time and they won't expect that you'll drop everything to attend to them at that very moment. They'll probably assume you're busy. But letting them know you're aware of their communication tells them you care. It lets them know they're important to you and that you're on it.

If you're nimble and responsive, you'll build up trust with others. They'll know you're somebody they can depend upon. Every time you respond, it's like you're placing a new deposit in a bank account of trust. And should there come an instance when, for whatever reason, you just can't respond promptly or with a response that's to their satisfaction (hey, we're all human), you'll have enough deposits built up that, hopefully, they'll be willing to let the matter slide. But trust can be fickle. Don't abuse your "trust" account.

Every time you respond, it's like you're placing a new deposit in a bank account of trust.

Effective communication is an ongoing thing. Sometimes, in our familiarity with someone—a customer or client or even a friend—we often take the relationship for granted. It's all too easy to let the communication basics slide after dealing with someone for a long period of time. Think about some of your best customers, for instance, the ones you've dealt with the longest. Are you still taking the time to thank them for their business? Are you still reacting quickly when they ask for something? Are you still trying to *earn* their business, in other words, with the same level of effort that you used when they first came to you? Remember how hard you probably worked for them in the beginning? Recall my examples about Rocco, the successful hair salon owner, or the donut shop that always gets the order right with a smile.

As long as you're doing some self-evaluation, take the time to consider your current relationships, both personal and business. Has your level of communication and responsiveness in general dropped off? Are you still working as hard to maintain your relationship and the trust you'd built up?

All of this, incidentally, presupposes a desire on your part to engage in or maintain any given relationship via communication. I'm not advising compulsory communication. No matter how nice we want to be, or how well we want to treat others, even complete strangers, you're never obligated to message or call someone back just because they want to talk or engage with you. Your time is valuable. Of course, not communicating is a form of communicating, too! Not replying to someone says that person isn't exactly high on your list of priorities. And that's okay, as long as that's your intention. That's your choice.

While you're considering how you communicate with others, how about taking a little time to examine the way you communicate with *yourself*. *Intra*personal communication is often as important as *inter*personal communication. What kind of positive affirmations do you give yourself? Pay attention to your self-talk. Is it negative and pessimistic and critical? Or is it positive and optimistic and self-reflective? We've all done it—treated ourselves worse than our worst enemy. As long as you're intent on treating others better, save a little effort for yourself.

Intrapersonal communication is often as important as interpersonal communication.

As with treating others well with manners, courtesy, and kindness, good communicating is a habit that you need to develop. And then maintain. You can't expect to be able to be a great communicator only during your working hours. Pay attention to how you engage with people in your personal life. Do you listen—really listen—to those around you? Do you respond promptly to them? Do you stop and think about how a text message to a friend might be interpreted before you send it? Are you being properly understood? The good habits you develop in your personal life will help you immensely in your professional life. Strive to be a good communicator *all the time.*

Once again, the key is awareness. This is the time for honest self-reflection. Your career trajectory, as well as your relationships with others, depends on it. I'm often asked about sales training. In turn, I always ask about communication skills. Communication mastery is a vital prerequisite to any kind of sales training. Indeed, it's a prerequisite to success. If I've communicated anything in this book, I hope I've communicated that!

SEVEN

GRATITUDE:
THE KEY TO FULFILLMENT

"The best time to plant the tree was twenty years ago.
The next best time to plant it is now."

– CHINESE PROVERB –

Earlier, I said that confidence and humility are two sides of the same coin. You need to be strong enough to know when you need to ask for help. Far from being a weakness, humility can be a great strength. In fact, I would argue that humility is necessary. If we can get our egos out of the way, if we can summon the courage to seek help when we need it, we can take giant leaps forward. Confident people aren't afraid to be humble.

In this chapter, I'd like to suggest another connection to humility: gratitude. We spend a lot of our time seeking ways to make our lives better and there is nothing at all inherently wrong with this. We all want better lives. We're all motivated by the promise of a better tomorrow. It's human nature to want to improve one's lot in life. But at the same time, this pursuit often makes us look right past what we have today. We take our current lives for granted. We think we deserve better, and we most certainly do! But sometimes, that ambition can blind us to what we have, even taking us to a point where we find ourselves complaining and grumbling about how "bad" things are. Even when, relatively speaking, they aren't.

But the humble person is the grateful person, grateful for what he has, and grateful for the opportunities that are before him to make his future even brighter. The non-humble person doesn't feel this gratitude. He feels a sense of entitlement instead, as if the universe owes him more. This sense of entitlement typically translates to a feeling of disappointment with what he's been given in life thus far. Frequently, he even becomes disappointed with success because no matter how successful he becomes, it's not enough. He feels that he needs more. Not "wants," mind you, but "needs." This level of disappointment leads to frustration and the frustration leads to a state of continual unhappiness and a lack of feeling fulfilled.

> The humble person is the grateful person, grateful for what he has, and grateful for the opportunities that are before him to make his future even brighter.

Dr. Robert A. Emmons of the University of California and Dr. Michael E. McCullough of the University of Miami did a study where participants were asked to jot down a few sentences each week. One group was asked to write down things they were grateful for and another group was asked to write down things that irritated or annoyed them. You can probably guess what happened. Ten weeks later, it turned out that the first group was much more optimistic and positive about their lives than the second group. Just a short little daily exercise—writing down some things they were thankful for—created a long-term change in their mental outlook. Surprisingly, this positive psychology even extended into their physical health, with the first group taking fewer trips to the doctor and generally reporting greater physical well-being.[1]

Many studies have replicated these results. Dozens, in fact. The connection is real. Do an internet search for "gratitude and happiness" and you'll find all the evidence you need. Grateful people are happier. Note that it's not the other way around. It isn't that these people are happy and, therefore, grateful. They're grateful and, therefore, happy!

> It isn't that people are happy and, therefore, grateful. They're grateful and, therefore, happy!

I'm not going to pretend that it's an easy thing to be grateful all the time. In the course of our day-to-day lives, it's easy to look past the good things we have. We get caught up in our work, we succumb to the stresses and pressures of our lives. We have bad days. Or weeks. We go through patches where it's tough to be

---

[1]   Emmons, Robert A., McCullough, Michael E., "Counting Blessings Versus Burdens: An Experimental Investigation of Gratitude and Subjective Well-Being in Daily Life," *Journal of Personality and Social Psychology*, 2003, Vol. 84, No. 2, 377–389.

positive about anything. Patches where nothing we do seems to make a difference.

Hey, I've been there. When I was thirty years old, I had recently just moved from Massachusetts to Maine with my first wife. I was still sorting out my future, trying to latch onto a decent career. My future seemed uncertain and unpromising. I didn't have a lot to be happy about, or so I thought, and my level of stress at that particular time in my life was sky high.

One Friday night, on our way to a holiday party for the company, my wife had just gone to work for, it all kind of came to a head. I felt out of sorts and miserable. The last thing in the world I wanted to do at that moment was mingle with strangers at a party, pretending to be happy and having a good time. All I wanted was to be alone. I had my wife turn the car around and take me home. She went to the party and I ended up having a full-blown panic attack in our apartment, the first of several that I would experience in my life.

While it was happening, I had no idea what was going on. All I knew was that I couldn't seem to catch my breath. I thought maybe I was having a heart attack. Soon, I felt as if I was going to die. I called 911 and an ambulance took me to the hospital where they ran a battery of tests and I learned my heart was fine. I had been overcome with a panic attack, something I'd heard of but had never had any firsthand experience with. Since that time, I have learned how to cognitively deal with these attacks. At times, I've been prescribed medication and there were certain lifestyle changes I made, too. But in the process of considering this attack, the main thing I asked myself was this: what kind of an outlook did I have on life that it would create underlying stress to a degree that would lead to a panic attack where I thought I was going to die? Surely, something was wrong with my perspective!

I don't want, for even a moment, to downplay mental health issues that may have more to do with chemical imbalances or other physiological factors. Anxiety and depression are very serious conditions that many people have, me included. If you're struggling with these issues, I encourage you not to waste any time in seeking the help of your physician or a qualified mental health practitioner.

That said, I will say that in my case, at that particular time in my life, my ability, or inability, to handle the stresses and strains of my life was a big factor in what happened on that Friday night and it had less to do with any underlying factors. The long and the short of it is that had I been in a better place psychologically—more *grateful* for what I had and for the opportunities that were surely out there in front of me, more positive, more hopeful, more optimistic, instead of so down and discontented—I probably wouldn't have had a panic attack. I probably would have gone to the party with my wife, met some very nice people, and had a genuinely good time.

Gratitude can be aimed at life in general, where you're grateful for the beautiful things we experience every day (sunsets, good health, chocolate-chip cookies—I'm sure you've got your own list) and gratitude can be aimed at the people in our lives. In your personal life, you cannot possibly thank enough those who are close to you, the people you love who collectively center you and provide an anchor for you. Your friends, your family, your significant other. Is there someone in your life you haven't thanked lately? What are you waiting for! You'll feel a lift in your spirits by doing so, and you'll certainly lift their spirits, too.

> You cannot possibly thank enough those who are close to you, the people you love who collectively center you and provide an anchor for you.

Professionally, expressing gratitude, the right thing to do in and of itself, has a very practical side benefit. People appreciate humility and gratitude. If you're thankful and openly grateful to the people who have helped you get where you are, they'll reciprocate in kind. When we accomplish something, some part of us always wants to think we were smart enough, or resourceful enough, or worked hard enough to make it happen all by ourselves. Most of the time, that's not the case, and deep down, we know it. Other people helped, and those other people need to be given credit.

Some people think it's a sign of weakness to admit that they needed someone's help to achieve this or accomplish that. On the contrary, it exudes power, grace, and maturity. It's all part of a winner's mindset, and it's necessary to keep moving onward and upward. If nothing else, expressing gratitude simply makes a person more likeable, even admirable.

> Openly appreciating someone's help is not a sign of weakness; it exudes power, grace, and maturity—part of a winner's mindset.

Being genuinely happy for someone else's success is another action sourced in humility, and another action that has a tendency to draw people toward you. Humble, grateful people appear more comfortable with themselves, more secure. They can be happy for the achievements of another because they're comfortable with themselves. They know that being happy for someone else doesn't minimize their own place in the world. Envious people, on the other hand, are insecure and that insecurity has a way of showing itself. You can spot it a mile away. It's not a very attractive trait, is it?

On the other hand, think of the people that you gravitate toward, the ones you find yourself wanting to help, or work with, or work for. Chances are they have that successful aura, that secure attitude where you can just tell by how they carry themselves that they've got it all together. They seem happy for themselves and they extend that happiness to those around them. There's rarely a hint of envy. They've got everything they need, and they're happy to see others get what *they* need. They're *winners*. The people who impress me the most are the people who have made it to the very top of their professions, yet remain gracious, approachable, and helpful. That's what winners look like!

Those with overinflated egos often forget the people who helped bring them success. Their lack of humility won't allow it. You can become rich and famous and even have streets named after you, but you must never forget those who were there for you during your rise. Don't allow those "streets" to be one-way! Gratitude is a two-way street. Be thankful for those who support you, and they'll be thankful to you.

It's an attitude. And if you don't have it, resolve to acquire it. Adopting an attitude of humility and gratitude is not difficult. It needn't be tied up in a complete personality makeover. Personalities can be hard to change, but attitudes are dynamic. Attitudes can change on a dime. Sometimes, it's just a matter of reminding yourself on a daily basis to be grateful, to be humble, to thank someone who's important to you.

Personalities can be hard to change, but attitudes are dynamic.

A GReat ATTITUDE = GRATITUDE. And for the most part, it's a matter of getting your ego out of the way. If you can do that, if you can be strong enough to be openly thankful for the help of others, to be grateful for what you have and the opportunities that are before you, to be humble enough to ask for help when you need it, you'll not only have that winner's mindset, you'll find, like the people in the study I referenced above, that you're happier. And I would go a step further: I'd say that you'll find yourself more *fulfilled*, which is beyond even happiness.

Very few people (if any) who are beholden to their own egos are fulfilled. We all know egomaniacs who appear to be successful, even Fortune 500 CEOs or high-level politicians or glamorous celebrities. You might have them in your own life. Without the humility to be grateful, however, it's very hard for these people to be fulfilled. Simply put, if you're not thankful, it's hard to be happy and satisfied. It's the wrong kind of success, an empty success that leaves the person with the inflated ego continually striving for more and more and more. He's on a hamster wheel, wondering why he's not getting anywhere, wondering why he's not feeling fulfilled. This is exactly what happens when you take gratitude out of the equation.

A healthy ego—your own sense of self-worth—is, of course, important. You won't get very far without it and I don't mean for a second to deny the importance of the ego. But think of it as a continuum, a question of degree. It's very hard for fulfillment and an unhealthy sized ego to share space in the same head. When an ego gets too big, it engulfs any chance of true happiness. Worse, the imbalance creates blind spots and the person with the oversized ego doesn't even recognize what's happening. It takes humility to see the need for a significant attitudinal change, and humility is the one thing the egomaniac doesn't have!

> It's very hard for fulfillment and an unhealthy sized ego to share space in the same head.

It's a form of denial and, in that sense, it's a lot like substance abuse. In fact, I would suggest that ego, improperly managed, has killed more people than alcohol or other drugs. An unbridled ego kills careers and relationships. It creates conflict, erodes relationships (home, work, and social), and eventually harms one's health and mental well-being. The comparison is not an idle one. Those seeking help for alcoholism often look to the famous twelve-step plan of Alcoholics Anonymous. If there's one common denominator in the twelve steps, it is humility. The steps involve such things as admitting to weakness, examining past errors, and making amends. It's a humbling process, the kind of process necessary to move forward once again with one's life. If you're ready to examine the management of your own ego, you could do worse than take a page out of AA's book.

In the end, the formula for fulfillment is a pretty simple one: Be humble, be grateful, be happy.

EIGHT

THE THING ABOUT LUCK

*"If you can meet with triumph and disaster,
And treat those two imposters just the same..."*

– RUDYARD KIPLING –

Before I took the call center job with Talk America that I discussed earlier, I had a job working the front desk at an exclusive health club for ten bucks an hour. This was after my time at the collections company. I had talked with my mentor, Paul Leary, about joining him in a company he had formed in Massachusetts with my other old mentor Peter Doolan, but for a variety of reasons, I wanted to stay in Maine. It was the right choice for me at the time, and so, until something better could come along, I took the health club job.

One day, sitting at the health club desk, I opened the newspaper and began scanning the want ads. That's when I saw the ad for Talk America. "Inbound phone calls, full training." The company sold self-improvement products and the top performers were making twenty-five to thirty dollars an hour, three times what I was making at the health club. Seemed like just the step-up that I needed.

I answered the ad and took the job. I loved it right away; I loved the phone interaction and the opportunity to sell. It really seemed to suit me. The work was hourly plus commission and until I could start making some decent money, I hung on to my job at the health club, working there during the day, and working a couple of nights a week at Talk America.

Soon, I started working at Talk America on weekends, an especially busy, and profitable, time period. Television infomercials would drive the calls and more people watched and responded on Saturdays and Sundays. They were more in a buying mood on weekends, too. One day, I noticed a poster in the call room: "Sales Contest. Top 15 agents will win a Caribbean cruise." By that time, I had done the math and knew that I could make a lot more money at Talk America than at the health club, so I gave my notice to the club and began working full time at Talk America. There were some 300 other agents manning the phones, and I was just a rookie, but I committed to winning that cruise. I figured I had just as good a chance as anyone. It was a ninety-day program and at the end of that ninety days, I finished at number ten and went on a very enjoyable vacation courtesy of the company.

I've already detailed a little of what came next. The job at Talk America eventually led me to become part of a start-up called PowerTel, which led to a partnership with my brother and others in a company called Triton, which led, ultimately, to early retirement. Of course, there were a lot of twists and turns and ups and downs along the way, but the interesting thing is that had I not noticed that ad in the paper way back when, I might have taken a decidedly different life track. What if I hadn't opened the paper that day? Or what if I had simply read right past it? None of what followed might have happened.

So, am I just the luckiest guy in the world, or what?

Well, luck is a funny thing. The fact is, many people responded to that same ad. I can only believe that many more people saw the ad, but failed, for one reason or another, to respond. Out of the ones who responded, many went to work just like I did. They had the same training. They sold the same products. Some worked the same number of hours, others worked much less. Some did very well, some did poorly. Most, as you'd expect, did average. Some stayed with it, some quit after the first day or got terminated along the way (some for not selling ethically). Some went on a cruise. Most did not.

What's my point? My point is that the ad represented an opportunity and nothing more. It might have been luck that I saw it, but a lot of people saw it. The difference is in what happened to us *after* we saw the ad. At that particular point in my life, after having experienced some success in a call-center environment in the collections business, and after whiling away the hours at a health club making ten dollars an hour, I was ready to break out. I was ready for success. The ad resonated with me; the *work* resonated with me. It felt *right*. It was the right moment for me, a moment I was mentally prepared for. So when the opportunity presented itself, I jumped all over it.

Looked at in that way, the events don't seem so lucky. Luck suggests randomness and haphazard chance. It might have been luck that I saw the ad, but I was ready to see it. I was ready for the opportunity. That's the key. Luck, as the Roman philosopher Seneca said, is where preparation meets opportunity.

> Luck is where preparation meets opportunity.
> —Seneca

What are you preparing for?

It's an important question. Luck and success are often misunderstood. They're often confused with one another. We see hugely successful people, people much more successful than we are, and right away we want to put their success down to luck. We're sure that with the same breaks, we could have been just as successful. Oh, sure, maybe they've got some raw talent, but probably they got a lot of lucky breaks along the way, too. Right? It's a perfectly human reaction to think this way. But it's wrong. Show me a lucky person, and I'll show you a person who was ready and looking for the opportunities that came his or her way, opportunities others probably missed.

Those opportunities are all around us. Everywhere and at all times. They are doors to a great future that we could simply walk right through if we could only see them. Now, your doors might be completely different than mine. The call-center environment worked for me. I liked the interpersonal communication and the sales aspect of it. It fit my personality. My soft skills, those intangibles we talked about earlier, made it a good match for me.

Conversely, had the job been, say, an engineering position, I would have been lost. It could have been the greatest engineering job in the world, but I wouldn't have lasted beyond day one. Since it probably would have required at least a college degree, I wouldn't have gotten past the resume screener in human resources! In fact, I wouldn't have noticed that particular door of opportunity to begin with. That door wouldn't be my door. But I took to the call center job, and the call center job took to me.

The secret to being prepared for opportunities, to see the doors that are right for you, is to know yourself—your strengths, your weaknesses, your likes, your dislikes. The things that excite you and make you want to get out of bed in the morning. We touched on it in Chapter 4: find something that excites you and you'll feel an inherent desire to succeed at it. Successful people have this kind of self-awareness and it helps them see the opportunities that are particularly suitable *for them*. They know what they want. They know what they're looking for. They maintain a constant level of preparedness, just waiting to come upon the door that has their name on it. That's a heck of a lot more than luck.

The secret to being prepared for life is to know yourself.

Unfortunately, what makes this process difficult is that we often get sidetracked by less important, secondary concerns. People often take jobs strictly for the promise of money, for instance, with little regard to whether they like the work or are even suitable for it. Entire careers are often forged like this. And then, many years down the road, the person wonders why every day seems to be a struggle and a complete grind, even if the financial goals are satisfied. If that sounds familiar, you might want to take some time to think about what really resonates with you.

Sometimes, people accept promotions, thinking a higher level of job is the answer, not fully realizing the responsibilities that may come with it. Sometimes, those responsibilities require enough additional work that the new salary, broken down, is less on a per hour basis than the original job! Promotions should be taken with the idea of learning and using new skills or for the long-term view of putting oneself on a more rewarding career track. Also, sometimes people take promotions that put them into leadership positions for which they're not skilled or don't really even want. Often, even a top performer at a lower level isn't qualified for an upper-level leadership position. If the skills you need for a promotion can be learned, and it's your desire to stretch yourself, then go for it. But know what it is you really *want* before you take a plunge.

I believe that money follows success no matter the field or occupation. Sure, some jobs naturally pay more than others, but if you're doing something you love, and something that fits your particular attributes, you'll do just fine. Maybe you can even find a way to do it through your very own company. With your own business, the sky is the limit.

Money follows success no matter the field or occupation.

If you're young and just starting out and you're having trouble finding your place in the world, welcome to the human race.

Starting out, we're all like that. I often think that's the entire purpose of your twenties—to figure out where you belong. It can be frustrating and discouraging, but it's perfectly normal. I experienced this firsthand. Before I found the collections job, I bounced around all over. I worked construction; I worked in a bank; I worked in a car wash; I tried corrections; and I gave the restaurant business a chance.

And why not? At that age, it's all fairly low risk. You haven't amassed a lot of wealth, so you don't have much to lose. Plus, you're probably living pretty cheaply. And the companies that hire you for entry-level positions aren't risking much either. They're probably not going to invest a lot in you unless, and until, they see that you're committed for the long haul. It's just one of those things that's understood in the working world. You're feeling them out, and they're feeling you out. It's okay to experiment like this. Trust me—eventually, you'll find whatever it is that resonates with you. If you're older than your twenties, that's okay, too. You're never too old to spend time figuring out what you want to do.

This doesn't mean that it's all smooth sailing once you find your calling. Guess what? No matter how unique your niche, there are probably thousands of people who are currently occupying it. Nobody's going to hand you anything. Welcome to the free market. Ah, but there are doors of opportunity here, too. If you're prepared for them, you'll see them. You'll find opportunities, and opportunities will find you. You'll get...luckier!

But just what does preparing look like? This gets us back to the other principles we've learned in this book thus far. It's about seeking help, finding mentors, having a winning attitude, treating others well, communicating effectively, and maintaining gratitude and humility. It's about the intangibles.

All of these things will keep you in the right place mentally for seeing and acting upon the opportunities that will certainly present themselves to you, sooner if not later. In the call center job, I was dedicated and committed. So much so, that I took the time to learn from the really successful people there. I approached a few of them and said, "Hey, I notice you're really selling the heck out of this new product. Do you mind if I plug into a few of your phone calls and listen in?" They were happy to let me and it helped me tremendously. I diligently studied the scripts we were given, too. I role-played with other agents. I worked hard. And the opportunities for success found me. It was like lighting a match.

People can be prepared for opportunities, and entire companies can be prepared for opportunities. It's the same concept. When we started Triton, we looked at our collective strengths and our collective weaknesses. We considered our aptitudes. Steve's major strengths, among others, were his business acumen and his ability to develop new business. My strengths were training the new hires, managing the call center, and delivering performance on the calls. Andy's strengths were in accounting and finance. The business, after some struggles, became successful because of the pieces we had in place. We would have failed without new business. We would have failed without effective call center performance on that business, as well as superior client service. We would have failed without the ability to manage the money. We were all suitable for our roles. We hired other capable people, too, and, consequently, we made the business work. We were prepared for success. We had ourselves lined up just right. And when the business opportunities came along, we were ready.

I mentioned the struggles. We had our fair share. I'm arguing in this chapter that you can make your own good luck, but that doesn't mean you're not going to experience some bad luck along the way, even if you do everything right. It happens, and more than we'd like to believe. One time, only in business a few years, we had a computer virus that made its way into our server-based telephony system and completely shut us down, almost putting us out of business. When you observe someone's or some company's success, you don't notice the hurdles that came before. But there's not a successful person or company in the world that hasn't been hit by something unforeseen at one time or another. Everyone experiences difficulties. Everyone experiences crisis situations. Everyone experiences bad luck!

But even bad luck can present opportunities if you're paying attention. We learn from our mistakes. For us, with the computer virus, we reconfigured our system support to ensure that we would never have to deal with a malicious computer attack again. We even made our security and systems redundancy part of our pitch to potential new clients. It helped us get contracts. Most importantly, we forged ahead, taking small steps, but moving forward just the same.

The fact is we all have to pay our dues. Remember: successful people don't normally start out as successful people. They limp along, feeling their way, making great strides one moment and then being pushed back the next. They pick themselves up, they move ahead a step or two, maybe fall down, then get back up once more. They keep moving. They abide by the intangibles, remain open to the opportunities that resonate with them, and find themselves, eventually, in a place of success. Bad luck, good luck, none of it matters. It's all about being ready. And that's the thing about luck.

There's not a successful person or company in the world that hasn't been hit by something unforeseen at one time or another. But even bad luck can present opportunities if you're paying attention.

NINE

PERSPECTIVE

"Life is ten percent what you make it and ninety percent how you take it."

— IRVING BERLIN —

So far, I've shared with you some of the things I've learned about how to be successful. In my coaching and mentoring work, that's obviously what most people want to talk about. "What can I do to be successful," or "What can I do to be *more* successful?" These are the questions I'm asked the most. Fewer ask about what to do when they come up against hardships, or impossible hurdles, or huge potholes, or what to do if the proverbial wheels just plain come off.

Part of this is because people have an unrealistic idea that if they do all the things they're supposed to do to succeed, they'll never have to worry about the bad times. Success means never having to worry about failure again. As if there's some plateau that, once reached, provides a lifetime of comfort without any worry. But another part of it is denial. We simply don't want to think about the possibility of bad times. Maybe if we don't think about them, we'll never be visited by them.

Unfortunately, life doesn't work this way. I can tell you this from personal experience. You're going to have rough patches *despite your best efforts*. It's an inevitability. You can do everything right and still have bad things happen to you. Most of the time, we can take corrective action and make things better. Sometimes, we can't. Sometimes, we experience a loss or a failure so significant that's there's nothing to do but hunker down and wait for time to make things right again. Maybe a lot of time.

Sometimes, what we need is not so much a means of correction as a means by which to more properly consider our situation, whatever it might be. What we really need is the right *perspective*.

You're going to have rough patches despite your best efforts. You can do everything right and still have bad things happen to you.

I learned this from one of the wisest people I have ever known: my mother. If you'll remember back at the beginning of this book, I spoke of an older brother whom I never got the chance to meet. David was killed riding his bike at the age of thirteen, before I was born. My sister, eleven at the time, was understandably despondent, hurting from the loss. Mom told her not to look at it as a loss. Mom told her to, "Think instead of the wonderful eleven years you had with David."

That's what I mean by perspective.

When I lost Jen, my mother was there with another golden nugget of perspective. "You'll never get over it," she told me. "You'll just learn to live with it." In time, I learned how right she was. I've never really gotten over Jen's death. Not entirely. Some part of me will always be tied to Jen. But I have learned to live with the loss. It took time, but the process was necessary.

Remember the actions I took not too long after the accident? I started dating again, looking, essentially, for a replacement. Looking for a way to get over something that I would never get over. It was a mistake.

My mother had the wisdom to know she'd never get over David's death. I came along not long afterward and my older siblings will tell you that my mother being pregnant with me was the first time since David's death that real happiness could be found on our parents' faces. There was a change in the way things felt around the house. Things seemed somehow lighter. But I was not a replacement for David. I know, because several times when I was just a kid, I asked Mom if that was the reason for me. "No, no, no," she would say emphatically. "You can never replace one child with another. It's an impossibility." I'm a father now, and so I know exactly what she meant. But the loss of David didn't mean she and Dad couldn't move forward with their lives, even as they would always have David in their hearts.

As I consider Mom's approach to life, the word that strikes me is "gratitude." Telling my sister to be grateful for the years she had David in her life is a good example. Being grateful for me and for her other children is another. We talked about this a lot in Chapter 7, but it's worth reiterating that the happiest people are not necessarily the people who have the most, but the people who are the most grateful for what they have.

> The happiest people are not necessarily the people who have the most, but the people who are the most grateful for what they have.

Part of being grateful for what you have means doing whatever you can to hang on to it. You'll still experience inevitable loss, but you'll hopefully decrease the amount of it. People who aren't truly grateful have a tendency to be careless with what they have, whether it's their possessions, or the close relationships that they take for granted. And when we're careless with things, we can easily lose those things.

For example, I worked hard to earn the money I made. I'm grateful for it.

I'm appreciative of it. Consequently, I take steps to maintain and grow it. But how many times have you seen someone come into sudden money—an inheritance or lottery winnings—only to see them lose it all as quickly as they got it? It happens all the time. It's estimated that one-third of lottery winners go bankrupt within five years. You see the same thing with people who inherit large amounts of money. Or businesses. A father works hard for years to create a successful company, dies, and his children run it into the ground within a year. It's not necessarily because the lottery winners or inheritors are stupid or inept; it's that they don't fully appreciate the opportunity the universe has given them. They're not grateful. They never had to work for the money and so they don't feel a strong enough connection to it. It's just a bonus that came into their lives.

I have learned that if you take care of your money, your money will take care of you. It's the same with anything, whether it's a home, a business, a friendship, or a marriage.

Whether it's money, possessions, or relationships, if you're careless with them, you'll lose them.

Bona-fide tragedies notwithstanding, sometimes we lose our perspective because we simply overreact to a loss or a setback. It's easy to do. In the midst of turmoil, it's hard to step back and look objectively at the situation and come to realize that, whatever it is, it's not really *that* bad. You've probably done it a thousand times: you get angry and stressed about something on Monday and find yourself laughing about it on Tuesday.

Bigger turmoils take more time to sort out. Maybe weeks instead of days. Maybe months instead of weeks. Maybe years. But most problems are almost never as bad as they at first seem. The same principle applies to triumphs and successes, by the way. They're almost never as good as they seem! If it's important to keep your perspective during the downtimes, it's also a good idea to keep your perspective during the good times. Neither will last forever.

Here's a common problem of perspective: sometimes, we end up disappointed in life because our *expectations* don't align with reality. Often, we set unrealistic goals. We start a new business venture and anticipate being on the cover of *Fortune* magazine after the first year. We start thinking about the company jet we're going to have. We imagine living in luxury. We have our mansion and yacht all picked out. When that level of success doesn't happen, is that a sign that we've failed? Or is it, instead, a sign that, just maybe, we ought to rein in our goals a little more? Maybe we're really winning when we think we're losing. Sure, there's always room for improvement, but we mustn't lose the perspective that success can only happen within the limits of reality. Imagination is a wonderful thing, but don't let it set you up for failure. Nothing is more demotivating than a goal that can never be hit.

On the other hand, something else that's demotivating is a goal that is *always* hit. Are you setting your sights too low? Are you coasting to your goals without breaking a sweat? An unrealistically high goal, or an unrealistically low goal, is just as bad as having no goal at all.

An unrealistically high goal, or an unrealistically low goal, is just as bad as having no goal at all.

Here's the thing you should know about goals: every goal comes with a corresponding sacrifice. The bigger the goal, the bigger the sacrifice. The sacrifice might be money, it might be time, or it might be both. In considering, for example, the lives of professional athletes, it might also be health. Think of retired NFL players suffering from the physical and, perhaps, mental effects of their careers—the pounding their bodies took on the field. What are you willing to sacrifice for your goal? There's no right or wrong answer, by the way. You might decide that working twenty hours a day is worth it to attain the goal, or goals, that you have in your sights. Or, you might decide that it's not, that you'd rather spend some of those hours on other things, like with your family. These are very personal decisions. I wouldn't begin to advise you on what your priorities should be. The larger point is that you have to know what the sacrifice is, and then you have to decide whether you're prepared to make it.

Every goal comes with a corresponding sacrifice. Are you prepared to make it?

George Doran, in a 1981 issue of *Management Review,* brought the acronym SMART into the lexicon of business language. What he described with the acronym is intelligent goal-setting and it looks like this:

Specific: Goals should be focused and targeted.

Measurable: There needs to be a way to quantify results.

Assignable: Who's responsible for the attainment of the goal?

Realistic: This is the one that trips up most people. A goal needs to be achievable.

Time-specific: What's a realistic deadline by which to achieve the goal?

The Institute for Professional Excellence in Coaching (iPEC) has since added an acronym to the front of SMART: AIM. The idea is to AIM SMART.

A = Acceptable minimum

I = Ideal

M = Middle

Sure, we all want to hit the ideal goal, but being realistic means knowing where the middle ground is. It's also important to know what the worst acceptable case is.

Intelligent goal-setting means realistic goal-setting and fewer disappointments.

Here's an example of goal-setting. One of my son's classmates recently took his PSAT and didn't score as highly as his parents thought that he should have. His father and I are friends and he confided in me that he was concerned enough that he talked to his son and demanded in no uncertain terms that he score much higher on the SAT. "I told him I wanted to see an improvement of 200 points on both math and verbal," he said. "Or else."

I didn't ask what "or else" meant. I said, "Is that realistic?"

My friend looked at me blankly and said, "What do you mean?"

I explained to my friend about AIM SMART. He had set a goal without even stopping to consider whether his son could accomplish it. That idea hadn't crossed his mind at all. The goal was certainly specific and measurable, but was it attainable? He confessed that he didn't know. I told him I thought it might be a good idea to do a little research. "Talk to his teachers," I suggested.

"Find out if his PSAT score represents true underachievement, an accurately representative assessment, or somewhere in between. Maybe there are certain things your son just needs to focus more on. Are there parts of the test he excelled at and other parts where he needs more work? If so, what are those parts where he needs the most help? Maybe he could benefit from some well-focused tutoring."

Armed with more information, my friend could set a more realistic goal. Now, it might be that an improvement in a score of 300 was realistic! For all my friend knew, maybe his goal was on the low side. Probably not, but how would he know without taking the time to better evaluate the situation?

I further suggested that it might be best to set an ideal goal, but also to know where the middle and minimum acceptable are. He could keep the latter two to himself and encourage his son to think only in terms of the ideal goal, but he needed to know himself what to realistically expect.

My friend's initial approach is the way in which most people go about setting goals in life. "I want to make six figures a year," they'll say. Or, "I want to become a millionaire." That becomes the goal. But just saying it won't make it come true any more than demanding a student get a higher grade on a test. You need to do more than simply declare a goal. You need to AIM SMART. By doing so, you'll know what to expect. You won't be surprised. You'll have a more realistic and better-defined *perspective* on your results.

Sometimes, we set not only the wrong level of goal but the wrong *kind* of goal. A lot of people will set income goals or status goals. I never have. I set performance goals for myself. How much business can I generate? How many sales can I close? How many hours can I work without getting burned out? Or, even more generally, what kind of career can I pursue to make sure I'm doing something I really like doing? Goals, in other words, that are specific *to me*, and not dictated by what society might think are worthwhile.

Here's what I've noticed: if you set goals true to yourself, the income will follow. I never concerned myself with getting wealthy. I just wanted to work productively at what I was good at. I wanted to do the best job I could do in my chosen profession. I wanted to be creative. I wanted to get up each morning and look forward to going to work. And guess what? I became wealthy. That's not a coincidence. It's perspective.

When all is said and done, perspective is how we make sense of life. I've had a couple of health scares over the years. The details aren't important right here, but believe me when I tell you that nothing focuses a person's perspective quite like the contemplation of one's mortality. It can be pretty sobering. It's no exaggeration to say that the way in which you look at life makes all the difference. Make sure you're looking at your life the right way for you. Be grateful, be ready for bad times, enjoy the good times, take care of what's important to you, be realistic in your expectations, set intelligent goals, and be true to yourself. If you view life with the right perspective, you'll be ready for anything at any time.

TEN

PAYING IT FORWARD

"When you learn, teach. When you get, give."

– Maya Angelou –

I've talked a little about the venture I started with my brother and other partners. Triton Technologies, Inc. was the company that ultimately propelled me toward early retirement. I also mentioned that it wasn't always clear sailing. There was that computer virus that almost put us out of business, along with a million other issues, some of which came at us completely unforeseen. Especially early on, it seemed that most days we were operating strictly in survival mode, just trying to keep the lights on. It was one crisis after another. I remember Steve saying, on more than one occasion, "We left three perfectly good jobs for *this?!*"

But through hard work and a lot of the principles we've already discussed in this book, we made the business succeed. I suppose if you had to point to something in particular that made us stand out, it would be our ethical guidelines. We did what we could to vet the clients, making sure the products we were selling for them were everything that they advertised them to be. This was very important to us. If they boasted about their refund policy, we made sure they lived up to it. We worked with products that we believed in and we were a better call center because of it.

There was something else, too. Some partners left and were replaced by new partners. Our clients' product campaigns had life cycles, too, and we had a fairly high turnover in the call center. But one thing that we did, regardless of product or employee or even partner change, bears mentioning here because we haven't really talked about it yet. No matter whom we brought in, our major focus was making sure they had something of real value to offer. Something we didn't already have. Our goal from the very start was to surround ourselves with talented people with a variety of skill sets. We did this as operating partners, with each of us approaching the business from a different background and with different talents, and we continued to do this as the business grew. Michael Dell put it like this: "Try not to be the smartest person in the room. And if you are, I suggest you invite smarter people or find a different room."

> "Try not to be the smartest person in the room. And if you are, I suggest you invite smarter people or find a different room."
> —Michael Dell

Six years after we started Triton, we had built it to a position where we could sell it for enough to be financially well set. But Steve and I stayed on for five more years to help the new owners take the business to an even higher level. I'm proud of the fact that Triton made *Inc* magazine's 5000

"Fastest-Growing Private Companies" list two years in a row and I'm equally proud of the fact that we were mentioned in Timothy Ferris's book, *The Four-Hour Workweek*. Ferris interviewed several different call centers for his book and interviewed Steve about including Triton in the section on the shortlist of phone sales centers to seriously consider. I credit a lot of our stellar reputation to the people we involved ourselves with—the people in the room who were smarter than us. The people who made us better with their knowledge and taught us things we didn't know.

This idea of learning from others is an idea I had a lot of time to think about once I retired. I've never been very good at sitting around doing nothing and it didn't take long for me to decide that I needed to do something useful with my time. Since I'd benefited so much from the education, goodwill, and guidance I had received from others, the idea hit me that I was in a position to benefit others with my own experiences. Hence, the idea of coaching and mentoring. It seemed like the natural next step in my life.

Coaching and mentoring, in other words, are ways that allow me to pay my success forward, and I'd like to suggest that if you've experienced success in your life, you find a way to pay it forward, too. Mentorship is, perhaps, the final leg of a person's career journey. Don't allow your knowledge and experience to go to waste. Put it to good use. Find a way to pass it along.

Mentorship is, perhaps, the final leg of a person's career journey. Don't allow your knowledge and experience to go to waste.

If you can make an income doing so, all the better. After all, even if you're retired like me, it is wise to take nothing for granted. There are very few fortunes that cannot be lost without care and diligence. Failed investments, illness, a market crash—there's no shortage of potentially unexpected pitfalls that can suddenly make a person's retirement pretty uncomfortable. And this, too, is a lesson. A big one. *There is no finish line.* Success is not a fixed place, but rather something that needs to be continually maintained. Success has to be earned every day no matter how successful you are. Don't forget the famous quote often attributed to Vince Lombardi: *"The only place where success comes before work is in the dictionary."* This is just as true after you've attained success as it is when you're working toward it.

Success is not fixed. There is no finish line.

Coaches, mentors, and consultants are always in demand. Knowledge is a valuable commodity. Information is like gold. It's essential to understand that being knowledgeable doesn't mean you have to be smarter than the person you're passing your knowledge along to. Knowledge and intelligence are two different things. This is important to recognize whether you're a mentor or a mentee. Anthony Robbins notes that "a coach isn't someone who is better than you. They just have a different perspective. Your coach will shift the game and show you how to get the results you want." It's the perspective that counts, the viewpoint of someone who can come in with a fresh set of eyes and consider your situation in a way you've perhaps never considered before.

So what am I saying? Simple: if you're looking to grow, find yourself a coach or a mentor as we discussed in Chapter 3. On the other side of the coin, if you have some knowledge you can pass along to others based on your own experiences and hard-won successes, pay it forward and become a leader, a mentor, a trainer, or a volunteer.

This idea of outside perspective is critically important. One of the more common things I've noticed in my time as a coach (and having my own coach), is how easily perspective is lost. I believe that the biggest reason for this is that in the day-to-day struggle to run a business or advance one's career, we often lose track of what we're struggling for in the first place. In the last chapter, we talked about goal setting. But before goal setting can even take place, we need to know what it is we ultimately want in life. This seems easy enough on the surface. We all want the same things—happiness and fulfillment, right? Ask anyone and that's typically the answer you'll get. So, why it is that so few people seem to be genuinely happy and fulfilled? Why is there such a disconnect between what people want out of life, and what they really have?

> A coach represents a fresh set of eyes to consider your situation in a way you've perhaps never considered before.

It has to do with that daily struggle idea. In the midst of the chaos of the day, with our typically overstuffed to-do lists, we don't take the time to think about what I call the quality of life questions. And even if we feel some vague notion that we ought to be spending more of our time contemplating those questions and making sure we're on track to get the things we really, truly want out of life (and not just those things that society tells us we want), we just don't ever seem to do so. We think that someday soon, we'll sit down and figure it all out. But even if we do sit down and try thinking these questions through, we often don't know how.

This is why even the best of us need coaching. We need that outside perspective. We need someone to help us explore our goals and desires, and to remind us of what we're working for, or ought to be working for. We need someone to help us stand back and see the whole forest.

Sometimes, this process can be frightening. There's always the possibility that we won't like what we see. There's a chance that we'll have to make major changes to how we're approaching life. We might discover that what we're doing isn't going to work in the long run. Change is not always easy. But the alternative is worse. The longer you travel down the wrong road, the harder it is to make a course correction. So find a way to examine *your* quality of life questions. Preferably with the help of an objective coach.

It's interesting to consider the origin of the word "coach." It wasn't until around 1830 that the word stood for anything other than a four-wheeled, covered carriage, like a stagecoach. But at Oxford University, it became a slang term for a private tutor who could "carry" someone through their exams. Soon, that particular meaning started being used in the world of sports. Now it refers to anyone who can help a person get where they want to go. The word, in a sense, still refers to travel, just like its origins. A good coach will guide you from Point A to Point B. Or, as I like to put it, from Point A to Point A+. It's often just a tweak here and there that leads to big rewards for the client. Coaching has been known to take functional clients and help them optimize certain areas of their lives.

A good coach will guide you from Point A to Point A+.

By the way, what's the difference between a coach and a mentor? Typically, the mentor has been there before us. He or she has knowledge regarding the best course of action to take to get the desired result or goal. The professional coach, on the other hand, partners with his or her client in a thought-provoking and collaborative way to inspire and empower the client, to push them to realize their full potential. The field of coaching as we know it today has really blossomed. This may be in large part because of numerous, easily researchable studies that point to the effectiveness of coaching for tangible betterment in one's personal and professional life.

Coach or mentor, if you're one of the fortunate ones like me who have made it through some rough times and come out of them a little wiser, then don't keep that wisdom to yourself where it's not doing any good. Pass it along. Be a coach or mentor yourself. Help people get where they want to go. And make the world a little better place.

ELEVEN

MOVING BEYOND "SUCCESS"

*"Do your own thing on your own terms
and get what you came here for."*

– OLIVER JAMES –

When I retired, I pretty much thought I had it made. I had won the game of life. After retirement and before my coaching and authoring career, I found myself with a lot of free time. This can be a blessing, but it can also be a curse. For me, without the imposed discipline of a work routine, little by little, I fell into some bad habits. I ate too much. I drank too much. I didn't take good care of my overall well-being.

This state of affairs ultimately brought on some health issues. Without going into too much detail, I was diagnosed with paroxysmal atrial fibrillation, a common heart rhythm disorder. Afib usually isn't immediately life-threatening, but I was told that the condition put me at a higher risk of stroke and over time could weaken my heart. In the course of diagnosing this condition, and through further imaging, the doctors also discovered I had a mildly-enlarged thoracic aorta, or aneurysm, as it's called.

The aorta is the large pipe that comes right from your heart. My modest thoracic aortic enlargement was likely caused by the heavy lifting I had done in my body-building days (and still continued to do into my fifties) along with not-so-well-controlled, high blood pressure. The combination of the straining from heavy lifting and the elevated blood pressure was, for me, the perfect storm that likely contributed to the aneurysm. In addition to being prescribed medication, I was told to slow down the drinking and to lose some weight, things that contribute to hypertension. I was never a daily drinker but would consume at unhealthy levels and it began to add up in terms of affecting my overall health, including my mental well-being. Also, controlling my blood pressure was essential for keeping the aortic enlargement stable.

Faced with the potential health and well-being ramifications, I did just that. In fact, I stopped drinking altogether. I also dropped a significant amount of pounds, and I began getting myself in better shape. Before long, I realized that I was feeling better than I had in years. I slept better, was more focused, and felt more drive and confidence, attributes that I had found in short supply on mornings after having had several drinks the night before.

But why did it take a potentially dangerous medical condition for me to begin caring about my overall well-being? I think it's because, for years, my focus was on other things. My work and my responsibilities as a father took up most of my time. I simply wasn't in the habit of looking after other segments of my life, like my health, as closely as I should have. Sure I'd go to the gym regularly and often eat healthily, but the poorly controlled hypertension exacerbated by the binge drinking was clearly not in my best interest and needed fixing before it became too late.

More to the point, I think that on some level, I confused my success in my career with success in everything. I was a "successful person." As such, I assumed *everything* about my life was good, including my health. But, of course, it doesn't work this way. Making enough money to retire early (or to at least take a sabbatical of a few years) wasn't going to do anything at all for my physical health. Or my family life. Or my spiritual life. Or any other segment of my life other than my financial well-being. After my health scare, I realized that all of these things had, to some degree, been neglected. I hadn't won the game of life, after all. I still had a *lot* of work to do.

Today, I consider myself fortunate to have received a warning shot across the bow. I took the warning seriously and made the necessary changes in my life. Wholesale, lifestyle changes can be tough, but usually worth the struggle. They certainly were in my case.

In 1954, psychologist Abraham Maslow published his famous hierarchy of needs concept. The hierarchy is essentially a pyramid with life's most basic needs—food, clothes, shelter—at the bottom, and self-actualization—realizing one's full potential to be everything he or she can be—at the very top. In between, from bottom to top, are safety, love and belonging, and esteem. As we go through life, whether we realize it or not, we're all trying to climb up this pyramid. When our basic needs are met, we move toward other needs. Eventually, if all goes well, we get to the top and realize our complete potential. In later years, Maslow allowed for another level beyond self-actualization that he called transcendence. This is when you go far beyond yourself, through altruism, for instance, or perhaps spirituality.

Not many people reach the level of transcendence, although I believe we can experience moments of it. I would argue that not many people reach the level of self-actualization, either, myself included. Indeed, can it be said of anyone that they have reached their "full potential" to be "everything" that they can be? How would that even be measured? And if it could be measured, wouldn't it be possible for someone at this mythical "full potential" level to go even one small step further? There is always room for improvement; there is always room for growth.

There is always room for improvement; there is always room for growth.

But this doesn't mean we shouldn't strive for self-actualization, even if the top of Maslow's pyramid is only theoretical. I mentioned in the last chapter that there is no finish line. Success is not a fixed place, but rather something that needs to be continually maintained. For a shot at self-actualization, we need even more than maintenance. We need to grow in all manner of directions—in our career, our financial situation, our health, our relationships, and in our spiritual life (whatever that might mean to you). This is the challenge all of us face all the time, no matter what level of success we've managed to attain. It's an ongoing process.

I went to work on all of these areas. My relationship with my son Alex was strong, but I worked to make it even stronger. I made sure to maintain a solid relationship with Joni, my ex-wife and Alex's mom. I kept myself in shape and paid closer attention to my diet. I worked to preserve the financial assets I'd acquired. And I made room for God in my life. For me, this simply meant thanking God every day for life, health, happiness, and prosperity. A prayerful "thank you" is perhaps the most basic yet important form of expressing gratitude.

As it happens, I discovered that there is a tremendous amount of overlap in these segments. I noticed that improvement in one area often meant a corresponding improvement in another. Preserving my financial capital allowed me a certain peace of mind that left me with more time and energy to spend on my relationships. Spending time with those I loved help feed my spiritual side. The parts of my life were connected. One fed into the other. What I learned is that the (never-ending) road to self-actualization is a holistic endeavor, involving the whole person, not just a part.

> The never-ending road to self-actualization is a holistic endeavor, involving the whole person, not just a part.

It's easy to forget this when we're in the midst of our daily life. Sometimes, we get hung up on the trappings of wealth, for instance. We work hard to earn money and, liking the results, we work harder to earn even more. Sometimes, this comes at the expense of the other areas of our lives. We end up like the hamster on the wheel. We're moving fast, but are we getting anywhere? Are we growing? Have we unwittingly sacrificed other parts of our lives? Are we self-actualizing?

Most of the time, we get tripped up by the most basic of human obstacles. We succumb to fear or anger or jealousy; we fall victim, in other words, to our own egos. Self-actualization means growing beyond these obstacles, growing beyond ego. Naturally, this is easier said than done. Everyone is human and everyone falls prey to fear and anger and jealousy and other negative emotions and influences. They're impossible to avoid!

What it comes down to is living life on *your* terms. This means taking charge of your life and going after the things that spell out self-actualization for you. Your approach and your goals may coincide with those of other people, or they may be completely different. The important thing is that they are *yours*.

You must never allow others to dictate the terms of your life. You can listen to others, you can take advice, you can observe how others go about their lives, you can look at things from a variety of angles (indeed you should do all of these things), but, in the end, the choices you make have to be your own and for your own ends.

Remember that, ultimately, you cannot hold yourself responsible for how others perceive you or receive you. Nor should you ever internalize any criticisms for doing what you want to do. Of course, you have a responsibility to be kind and respectful to others, but you also have the right to live on your own terms unapologetically and without explanation. This might require certain boundaries. Friends or relatives, or even a significant other, might have expectations for you that you have no interest in. It's not easy to reject the expectations of others, but living by them is much worse, leaving you potentially frustrated, resentful, and angry.

Never allow others to dictate the terms of your life.

Getting to the point where you're comfortable with what you're seeking in life requires that you develop and maintain your *awareness* of those factors that are constantly influencing you, whether they are internal feelings or external forces. You can feel anger, for instance, without allowing it to control you. Are you letting your envy persuade you to make a decision that you wouldn't otherwise make? Do you really need that expensive suit, or are you buying it because your coworker has one just like it?

In other words, what are your motivations? Awareness means knowing *why* you're doing *what* you're doing. Stop and think about whether you're allowing your ego to call the shots. Are you operating on your own terms, or are you operating from a place of envy or anger or in accordance with the expectations of others? The answer requires genuine awareness.

Awareness means knowing why you're doing what you're doing.

Being aware means understanding that your actions are a matter of personal choice. Are you going through a hard time? Are you depressed by your circumstances, paralyzed by doubt and uncertainty? Are you listening too much to others, even if what they are saying conflicts with your inner thoughts and ideas? If you're not aware of any of these feelings, it's easy to allow them to control your actions, even to control who you are.

An important distinction, however, has to be made between controlling the various events of life and controlling your responses to those events. The latter are in your grasp. The former? Well, not so much. Many people have the idea that if they just do everything right, their lives will be perfect. If I've learned nothing else in my own life, I've learned the fallacy of this idea. Things happen and sometimes those things are bad. No matter what we're striving for, we can control our efforts but we can't control the outcome.

I've dealt with anxiety in my life and I've seen it in others. I can tell you that a lot of anxiety comes from too much of an attachment to outcomes. Too much attention to what cannot be controlled. Focus on what you can control instead. Focus on the effort.

Control your efforts. The outcomes will take care of themselves.

Indeed, knowing and focusing on what's within your control, and knowing and accepting that which is not within your control, is a big part of personal development, maybe, when all is said and done, the biggest part. Interestingly, over-attachment to outcomes can work against you even more when things are going well. We've all seen it: someone gets lucky, pays way too much attention to the (fortunate) outcome, and rests on their laurels. The efforts become secondary. The person only remembers the outcome. And then the next outcome frequently isn't so great. Ask any musician who's produced a one-hit wonder. Or the salesperson who was handed an important account that initially brought him a lot of commission dollars. The lack of effort to acquire new accounts becomes painfully obvious down the road when the dollars dry up! The outcomes, good and bad, will present themselves all in good time. All you can do is pay attention to your efforts *now*.

Work hard, but work hard on the things that resonate with *you*. Live life on your terms. Be aware of those internal and external influences that have the potential of derailing your plans. They're out there and you have to watch for them.

Most importantly, pay attention to all of the segments of

your life that, together, make up who you really are. Move toward self-actualization. And if you think you're there, keep on going!

TWELVE

RESILIENCY, GUTS, AND GRIT

*"Do not judge me by my success, judge me by
how many times I fell down and got back up again."*

– NELSON MANDELA –

When I was still fairly young, something very important occurred to me about my future: I was going to have to work hard at it. I was not blessed with enough athleticism to become a pro athlete. I was not blessed with enough intelligence to become a neurosurgeon. I had no acting ability nor connections in Hollywood. I didn't have a rich uncle anywhere and I was not the next-in-line for control of a prosperous family business. Whatever success I was looking for, it probably wouldn't come easy.

If you're like me, you probably recognize these disadvantages in your own life. But I discovered something, as I hope this book has made clear by now. These aren't disadvantages at all, really. Not in the world of business and entrepreneurship. The world of entrepreneurship comes with an even playing field. Anybody can join in and anybody can compete. You don't need to be super intelligent or highly educated or well-resourced. Earlier, we talked about the *intangibles* and it's worth bringing them up again. Things like competitiveness, focus, confidence, humility, enthusiasm, commitment, dedication, and hard work. Anybody armed with these characteristics can be a success. I don't believe these qualities can be learned, but I do believe they can be nurtured and cultivated. And I don't think you'd be reading this book if you didn't possess these intangibles to some degree.

Plain and simple, that means you can be a success. I did it and what one person can do, another can also do. Starting out, I had nothing more than you have now. I had the intangibles. Always remember: *Tangible results come from intangible qualities.*

As a matter of fact, you may even have less than what I had when I started, or at least what I had to deal with twenty years ago. I'd lost my fiancé. I'd lost my mother. I was facing bankruptcy. I had to pawn possessions to make ends meet. But I went from despair to millionaire, something I couldn't have imagined at the time.

> The world of entrepreneurship comes with an even playing field. Anybody can join in and anybody can compete.

But I also couldn't imagine failure. I was determined. I didn't know how far I'd get, but I knew I was going to keep going, keep putting one foot in front of the other. Looking back over the last couple decades, I can now see that success was all about the "bounce." Everyone has hard times. Everyone has setbacks. Not everyone bounces back, but I contend that that has more to do with those intangibles than anything else. The intangibles create results and they also produce resiliency during those times when the results aren't coming. In fact, in my coaching, I call myself a resiliency coach, rather than a success coach. Success, I have learned firsthand, doesn't come without resiliency.

Success doesn't come without resiliency.

It also won't come without guts and grit. My mentor Paul Leary would often say, "It takes guts to make a profit." If there's another intangible that we haven't discussed yet, it's this one. Success almost always involves risk. You have to risk time, money, or, most commonly, both. Some people are risk-averse. Other people are gamblers. Gamblers don't necessarily have guts. It's in a true gambler's nature to take risks. He gets a kick out of it. Real guts means proceeding forward even if a large part of you wants to bail out. So if you're feeling anxious or nervous about a venture, that's okay. That's normal. Moving forward *in spite* of your fears is what guts is all about.

It takes guts to make a profit and moving forward in spite of your fears is what guts is all about.

A lot of times, fear comes from within. In other words, it's not that you have doubts about whether a particular venture will work. It's that you have doubts about whether *you* can make it work. As if you're not the right person to carry it out. We all feel this. I had doubts about finishing this book. (And yet here you are reading it!) It's surprisingly common. There's even a name for it. Psychologists talk about "Imposter Syndrome." Fortune 500 CEOs have been known to experience this. It's a feeling that, no matter how successful you appear and no matter your accomplishments, you'll one day be exposed as a fraud. It's a feeling that you're living a sort of lie, as though deep down you don't deserve success. If you've ever felt this self-doubt, you're in good company. A list of others who have reported some level of imposter syndrome in their lives includes Neil Armstrong, David Bowie, Serena Williams, Lady Gaga, Maya Angelou, and Tom Hanks. For these people, guts meant putting those fears of being a failure aside and pushing on through. There's no critic quite as destructive as the inner critic. Stop listening so closely to your inner critic. Maybe you can't stop hearing it, but that doesn't mean you have to buy into its doubt.

In my own experience, I've learned that a strong support system is extraordinarily helpful in this regard—friends and family, of course, but even a network of like-minded acquaintances, people with similar ambitions who are facing the same kinds of hurdles that you are. Such a group can help you gain valuable perspective and remind you that you're not alone, that everybody has stumbling blocks, both external and internal. People network to find new business, which is terrific. But networking to have a support group to lean on is just as valuable.

When I'm particularly down, I'll work out. A good cardio workout helps release those endorphins and gets me out of my low-energy funk. Lately, I've also been keeping a gratitude journal. This has helped me de-emphasize the negative and emphasize the positive things in my life. We talked about gratitude back in Chapter 7. What are you grateful for? Find at least one thing a day and jot it down in your journal.

You have to feel good about yourself on a personal level, too—the way you treat others, the kind of person you want to be, notwithstanding whatever success you might attain. And how you treat yourself is important. I felt better after I stopped drinking, started eating healthier, lost forty-plus pounds, and got myself in better physical shape. Take care of yourself physically and the mind will follow.

Maybe the most powerful exercise to lift you up when you're down is to remember the *why*. Often, we get so caught up in the everyday pursuit of our goals that we forget why we made them in the first place. We forget what we're working for! Take some time to review your aspirations. Imagine success. Keep your eyes on the prize. Become re-inspired. Nothing is more motivating than knowing exactly where it is you want to go.

A word has to be said about gutting something out long after it's reasonable to do so. Sometimes, the wise thing is to know when to cut one's losses. If something isn't going to work, it isn't going to work. No amount of motivation or resilience or grit or guts can take a venture doomed to fail and make it a success. This is often a hard thing to accept. Nobody wants to be thought of as a quitter. The mistake, however, is confusing quitting with personal failure. Quitting doesn't mean you failed or that you are a failure. It only means that you tried something, gave it your best shot, and then determined it was in your best interest to move onto something else.

> Imagine success. Nothing is more motivating than knowing exactly where it is you want to go.

Smart businesses do this all the time. They do it with metrics, analyses, surveys, or whatever else necessary to judge their efforts in a quantifiable way so as to determine the future of some particular undertaking. If you're banging your head against a wall because you're afraid of being "a failure," then you're listening only to your own ego. That's a poor place to find quantifiable information that can help you make smart decisions. If you're struggling with a particular endeavor, investigate the struggle in an objective way and determine whether it's worth continuing, or time to move on to something else.

If you determine that it's worth pursuing, then give it all you've got. Look for success stories of similar ventures and find a way to learn how they did it. If they could to it, so can you. Remember the even-playing field of entrepreneurship. Implement those intangibles that are already a part of your psychological make-up. Go at it with guts and grit. Be resilient. You'll need to be for the inescapable setbacks. But you'll get there. I'm living proof.

FINAL THOUGHTS

When I started writing this book and telling others about my plans to publish it, I had no idea there would be so much interest in it. The interest, I quickly determined, was not because I had any big secrets of success to share, but because there's a general hunger for helpful information. We're all looking for ways in which to make our lives and our careers better. We want tomorrow to be better than today. It's a human desire to want to strive for improvement, to move toward some ideal of personal or professional success. Guidance from someone who's attained some level of that success is always welcomed.

But this left me feeling a bit intimidated. I felt a big responsibility to make sure my advice was worthy of the time someone would need to invest to read it. Fortunately, as I proceeded, I gained more and more confidence. The principles of success you just read about are tried and true. I can use myself as Exhibit A, but I think you can find a lot of examples out there of people who have lived by these ideas and had at least some degree of success. I mentioned in the very introduction to this book that much of what followed was common sense. I don't imagine I've written anything that struck you as totally new. I'm not sure that there *is* anything new out there. The problem most of us have is not a failure to learn, but a failure to remember.

If this book has helped you to remember the power of goal-setting, or the power of the intangibles, or the power of effective communication, then I will consider it a success. Now, all you have to do is apply these ideas to your own life. I know that you can. I know, because successful people do the thing that you just finished doing—they read books like this one. Or they attend seminars or listen to podcasts or talk to mentors or coaches. Successful people are always looking for ways to improve. That describes you.

I want to thank you for your desire to improve. If everybody had that, this world would be a much better place. I want to thank you for reading and I want to wish you the best of luck going forward. But I also want to wish for you the resilience to bounce back even in the face of bad luck, even all the way back from despair. I know firsthand that it can be done. In fact, it might be worth mentioning that even as the final touches were being put on this book, I experienced a fairly significant setback. I suffered a detached retina. Thanks to the skill and expertise of my eye surgeon, my vision was saved. However, I needed emergency surgery that required weeks of recovery, including a full week where I had to remain in a face-down position with limited computer-screen time. With the loving support of family, the encouragement of colleagues eager to read the book, and my own steadfast commitment, I finished the book from that face-down position, having my editor read to me so that I could make the final edits. What kind of resilience coach would I be if I didn't practice what I preach?

One last thing: I'm always interested in feedback and in hearing success stories. And I'm always available in my role as coach to help out if I can. Feel free to connect with me. I'd love to hear how your journey is going. Like most journeys, I imagine yours has its share of ups and downs. Be grateful during the ups, hang in there during the downs. In the end, I know you'll find all of it worthwhile.

POINTS TO PONDER

Chapter 3
Mentors: Pathways to Success

There are people out there who have knowledge that you can use. People who can save you a lot of time and heartache.

To find a mentor, you have remain open, coachable, teachable, and willing to learn and better yourself.

The people that I learned from, smart as they were, weren't magicians or miracle workers. They just happened to have the right knowledge, and that knowledge was replicable.

Deciding you need a mentor requires some humility, an open admittance to yourself that you don't have all the answers. And to know that the key is to find the people who do.

The best way you can pay back a mentor is to pay it forward. Be a mentor yourself!

Chapter 4
The Intangibles

A winning attitude is not just positive thinking. It's more than that. It's all of those little characteristics, like commitment and dedication and enthusiasm and hard work.

It's impossible to manufacture competitive fire out of thin air. If you're doing something that you just can't get yourself excited about, then you need to find another pursuit.

Successful people have the humility necessary to learn. And the confidence to allow themselves to be humble.

Tangible results come from intangible qualities.

If you're stuck, check your level of motivation.

Chapter 5
Treating Others Well

These days, it seems we're all out of touch with our fellow world travelers and, consequently, we're out of practice in dealing with them.

It doesn't cost you anything to be nice!

Don't wait for a good mood to smile. Smile and allow the good mood to follow!

How aware are you of your own behavior? From time to time, we could all use a moment to look in the mirror and see if we're the kind of people we want to be.

If you can separate yourself from your competition with courteousness and professionalism, you'll have all the advantage you'll need.

Chapter 6
Communication

The ability to effectively communicate is not an option for anyone seriously engaged in furthering their career.

The most important part of communication—listening—is the most overlooked.

Our ability to communicate is so vitally important because it's one of the main things that people judge us by, and certainly one of the first.

Nobody is born as a great communicator. The good news is that communication skills are learnable!

Every time you respond, it's like you're placing a new deposit in a bank account of trust.

Intrapersonal communication is often as important as interpersonal communication.

Chapter 7
Gratitude: The Key to Fulfillment

The humble person is the grateful person—grateful for what he has and grateful for the opportunities that are before him to make his future even brighter.

It isn't that people are happy and, therefore, grateful. They're grateful and, therefore, happy!

You cannot possibly thank enough those who are close to you, the people you love who collectively center you and provide an anchor for you.

Openly appreciating someone's help is not a sign of weakness; it exudes power, grace, and maturity—part of a winner's mindset.

Personalities can be hard to change, but attitudes are dynamic.

It's very hard for fulfillment and an unhealthy sized ego to share space in the same head.

Chapter 8
The Thing About Luck

Luck is where preparation meets opportunity. —Seneca

The secret to being prepared for life is to know yourself.

Money follows success no matter the field or occupation.

There's not a successful person or company in the world that hasn't been hit by something unforeseen at one time or another. But even bad luck can present opportunities if you're paying attention.

Chapter 9
Perspective

You're going to have rough patches despite your best efforts. You can do everything right and still have bad things happen to you.

The happiest people are not necessarily the people who have the most, but the people who are the most grateful for what they have.

Whether it's money, possessions, or relationships, if you're careless with them, you'll lose them.

An unrealistically high goal, or an unrealistically low goal, is just as bad as having no goal at all.

Every goal comes with a corresponding sacrifice. Are you prepared to make it?

Intelligent goal-setting means realistic goal-setting and fewer disappointments.

Chapter 10
Paying it Forward

"Try not to be the smartest person in the room. And if you are, I suggest you invite smarter people or find a different room."

—Michael Dell

Mentorship is, perhaps, the final leg of a person's career journey. Don't allow your knowledge and experience to go to waste.

Success is not fixed. There is no finish line.

A coach represents a fresh set of eyes to consider your situation in a way you've perhaps never considered before.

A good coach will guide you from Point A to Point A+.

Chapter 11
Moving Beyond "Success"

There is always room for improvement; there is always room for growth.

The never-ending road to self-actualization is a holistic endeavor, involving the whole person, not just a part.

Never allow others to dictate the terms of your life.

Awareness means knowing why you're doing what you're doing.

Control your efforts. The outcomes will take care of themselves.

Chapter 12
Resiliency, Guts, and Grit

The world of entrepreneurship comes with an even playing field. Anybody can join in and anybody can compete.

Success doesn't come without resiliency.

It takes guts to make a profit and moving forward in spite *of your fears is what guts is all about.*

Imagine success. Nothing is more motivating than knowing exactly where it is you want to go.

ACKNOWLEDGMENTS

There are many people to thank for this book. I suppose the place to start would be my parents, who taught me many of the intangibles.

Thank you to my brother Steve, a mentor and best friend.

My sister Bonnie has been a constant source of support and encouragement.

Endless gratitude to my son Alex who makes me so proud to be his father.

My thanks to all the members of my family; each has taught me something valuable in their own way.

Thank you to Joni, who has been a devoted mother.

Paul Leary, Sr. and other mentors mentioned herein are owed a special thanks. I hope it's enough to pay forward your lessons in this book.

Much gratitude goes out to the early reviewers of this book who, with their wonderful endorsements, provided me the encouragement to see this project through.

Thanks to Janet Shapiro and the team at Smith Publicity for their hard work and valuable direction.

Finally, my appreciation to my editor, Jerry Payne, for his dedication and for helping me get the words right.

ABOUT THE AUTHOR

Certified by the Institute for Professional Excellence in Coaching (iPEC), Eric Chasen is a mindset and resiliency coach. Early in his career, he suffered personal and professional setbacks that sunk him to the depths of despair. His amazing turnaround, comeback, and ultimate success propelled him into the world of coaching and mentoring. *From Despair to Millionaire: Growing Beyond Hardship* details his personal journey while outlining his secrets for success and for life.

Eric lives in Massachusetts where he spends quality time with his son, at the gym, writing, or helping others reach new levels of professional and personal excellence.

Connect with Eric at *www.ericchasen.com.*

CPSIA information can be obtained
at www.ICGtesting.com
Printed in the USA
LVHW040442210820
663573LV00004B/177